'Dave Kitchen is a genius! He has a knack for helping eyes. Dave's great insight is that he knows that there is a being outside a story and inside one. His talent is to prese stories of the Bible in a way that enables us to enter them in our imaginations. As we get inside the story, we notice things we never noticed before; the stories become richer, deeper and more meaningful. This book is a great resource for Christians and churches to use during Lent. It is also accessible for readers with no prior knowledge or experience in reading the Bible. The Easter story has been one of the foundational stories of western civilisation, here we have a resource that will help people to enter that story, to feel its significance and meaning, and, even more excitingly, to explore what their own response to that story might be!'
**The Revd Stephen March, pioneer priest in Leicester Diocese**

'The greatest story ever told with an invitation to not just read it – but step into it. Get ready for an incredible journey.'
**Rob Parsons, founder of Care for the Family**

'In this very helpful book, David Kitchen brings us imaginatively into the events of Holy Week and Easter through a wide variety of witnesses. There is new insight on every page. Both individual readers and those who lead worship or study groups will find much to inspire.'
**The Revd Donald P. Ker, former secretary and president of the Methodist Church in Ireland**

'Dave Kitchen has done it again. Having brought characters from scripture to life in *Bible in Ten*, *Easter Inside Out* does the same for the most significant week in history. If we ever forgot that Easter was about real people at a real time in a real country, *Easter Inside Out* reminds us in a lively, readable, creative and captivating way.'
**The Revd Dr Jennifer A. Hurd, chair of Wales Synod Cymru**

'Dave Kitchen has been getting inside the hearts and minds of the first followers of Jesus and those he encountered for more than 50 years, enlightening and inspiring so many people through in the process. Now he has done it again with *Easter Inside Out* in which we are invited to journey with Jesus and those who knew him from Palm Sunday to Good Friday and then to Easter and beyond. Suitable for personal reflection and devotion, it will also make an excellent small group resource during Lent or even as a one-off book group read, with stimulating questions provided for both.'
**The Revd David Mullins, retired Methodist minister**

'Holy Week is the most significant week in the Christian faith that has literally transformed the course of human history. Dave Kitchen approaches the gospel stories of this crucial week with creativity and imagination. In a series of vignettes, he brings the story to life and locates the overarching narrative on the hustling and bustling streets of Jerusalem. He does so in a way that is always accessible and engaging. It is my hope that *Easter Inside Out* would enable anyone to think afresh about this story and the impact it can have on our lives.'
**The Revd Andrew Charlesworth, chair of Wales Synod Cymru**

'*Easter Inside Out* does exactly what the tag line says: it's a fascinating retelling of the Easter story as if you were there. David weaves together biblical and imagined characters to take the reader through the events of Easter week in their own words, bringing them to life as they deal with all the ups and downs of their being part of the days that changed the world. A detailed timeline helps the reader keep pace with the fast moving moments. David has given us a truly original version of the greatest story.'
**Roger Aubrey, PhD, MTh, writer and international Bible teacher**

# EASTER INSIDE OUT

**BRF** Ministries

15 The Chambers, Vineyard
Abingdon OX14 3FE
+44 (0)1865 319700 | brf.org.uk

Bible Reading Fellowship is a charity (233280)
and company limited by guarantee (301324),
registered in England and Wales

ISBN 978 1 80039 351 6
First published 2024
10 9 8 7 6 5 4 3 2 1 0

**Acknowledgements**
Every effort has been made to trace and contact copyright owners for material used in this resource.
We apologise for any inadvertent omissions or errors, and would ask those concerned to contact us
so that full acknowledgement can be made in the future.

A catalogue record for this book is available from the British Library

Printed and bound in the UK by Zenith Media NP4 0DQ

# DAVID KITCHEN

# EASTER INSIDE OUT

## THE STORY AS IF YOU WERE THERE

**BRF**
Ministries

*For Reuben and Leni, the next generation*

# Contents

## THURSDAY

## FRIDAY

## LATER

# It starts like this

I'm about fourteen. It's Easter again and a preacher is telling me how *wonderful* it would be to have been there on that very first Easter morning. I think I know what the preacher means by this. What an astonishing story to actually be a part of!

But *wonderful*? Terrifying might be closer to it. Remarkable, perhaps, but also disturbing. Definitely puzzling and troubling too.

Looking back from thousands of years later, we know how it all turned out. But when you're living it, you don't have that perspective. Looking back, we can relate in a way no one ever does in the heat of the moment.

Five hundred years ago, Christians like Ignatius of Loyola would make it part of their Bible study to try to bring a part of the gospel story to mind and to life by putting themselves in the situation they were reading about. It's an ancient and important part of getting to know and understand the Bible, but we don't use it as much as we might.

I've now spent the best part of a lifetime retelling bits of the Easter story in one way or another. One of the radio programmes I co-wrote even won an award for bringing three of the characters to life. It was a feel-good moment even if I wasn't sure I deserved it.

But what I've never done until now is explore ways that the story fits together as a whole from the various accounts. A couple of years back, I decided to see if I could get a good sense of what it must have been like, day by day, as the Easter story unfolded. Is there enough information to reconstruct that in a reasonable way from what we know?

A few wise heads told me I might not actually be able to do such a thing. That was just the encouragement I needed! Of course, after 2,000 years, people can always choose to draw slightly different timelines. But everything I've described here is based on the evidence or is a reasonable assumption that can be drawn from that evidence.

So, if you want to feel Easter as if you were there, to experience it from the inside out, to sense what it might have been like to live through those days, then this is the book for you.

> To start, let's set the scene: it is the week of the Passover and everyone seems to be in Jerusalem. After quite an absence from the city, it's rumoured that Jesus from Galilee is planning to be one of the visitors.

# PALM
# SUNDAY

# Dangerous or religious:
## Albus, soldier at the city walls

I was stationed in the guard-house tower that afternoon. So almost certainly I was the first to get a glimpse of what was happening.

'Some sort of party or it could be a religious ceremony coming our way,' I yelled down to my commanding officer.

'Dangerous or merely what you'd expect in this land?' Quintillus shouted back up.

I heard the thump, thump, thump of his footsteps as he came up to join me. The group was a bit closer now and I could make out a man who appeared to be on horseback at the centre of it all. Suddenly it didn't look too good. I smelled riot and revolution.

Quintillus hauled himself up the final couple of steps. He squinted into the middle distance and said, 'Well, what do you think it is?'

'Looks to me like a "hero" returning to make a nuisance of himself during the holiday season. What's this one?'

'Passover.'

'Well, it would be better if they all passed over and left us in peace. If that bloke is on horseback, I reckon we need the legion out now.'

Quintillus sighed. He hated fuss. 'Just keep the peace,' he used to say. 'That's what we're here for.'

'Look more carefully, Albus.'

'Ah, he's side-saddle on a donkey.'

'Exactly. Most military leaders don't ride in on animals used for carrying sacks of grain, do they? And can you see any sign of weapons hidden under the folds of what they're wearing?'

'Not so far.'

'Well, keep looking because there's a chance that it will turn nasty, but I don't see any sign of it at this moment. What do you think it looks like right now?'

'More like an open air dance party. Seems a bit peculiar to me.'

'Have you picked up nothing about this religion since you were posted here, Albus? Their scriptures are full of song and dance. Even their old kings used to do it.'

'Doesn't sound anywhere serious enough to count as religion in my book.'

'Ah, that's where you're wrong. This is a religion filled with passion, fire and even dance. That's why our job here is a bit trickier because they feel for their faith more powerfully than in some of our territories. It can get out of hand pretty quickly.'

'So we stamp on it, sir.'

Quintillus sighed. 'Our job is to keep the peace and collect the taxes. That's what Rome wants and that's what Rome will get. If you see weapons or horsemen, just tell me and I'll have soldiers here on the double to remove the ringleader's head from his body if necessary. In the meantime, they can sing "Hosanna" as many times as they wish and dance until dusk. What harm can it do? Have you never called on your gods to save you?'

'I would if I thought it would do any good.'

'Well, keep watching, Albus. You might even learn something.'

And, with that, he turned and plodded back down the stairs leaving me to watch and wonder about what sort of saving this group were expecting from this strange god of theirs.

## Where to find this story in your Bible?

- Matthew 21:1–11
- Mark 11:1–10
- Luke 19:28–38
- John 12:12–16

# Looking over the edge:
## Thomas follows instructions

It was extraordinary. No other word for it. None of us had any expectation we were going to draw a crowd of that size and it felt spine-tingling – the noise, the laughter, the cheering. I thought to myself: now this is truly what I call a festival.

But, as Jerusalem came into view, I noticed the guard-house high in the city wall. People call me a pessimist, but I've always argued that I'm a realist. When you're in the middle of a parade which has turned into an amazing outdoor party, somebody should be watching out for the people who might break it up.

Things had begun to go a little crazy when the crowd started cutting down palm branches to wave at Jesus as if he was lord and master of everything he surveyed. That was thrilling, of course, because it looked as if we were going to change the world.

Yet I spotted the guard-house. I think, deep down, I doubted that this was actually the start of a glorious new chapter. Part of me wondered whether it was something darker.

I knew how dangerous Jerusalem was. And Jesus had said plenty about suffering and death. Nobody who listened closely to him could end up with the impression that life was going to be easy.

That morning Simon Zealot and I had been given the task of collecting a colt for Jesus to ride on. The instructions were exact and they included a sentence to say if we were challenged: 'The Master needs it and will send it back shortly.' The reason seemed clear enough to me. Jesus didn't want news of his arrival reaching Jerusalem before he did. Enemies needed to be on the back foot if it was at all possible.

The distance between Bethphage, where his ride began, and Jerusalem itself is no more than a mile or two but the crowd just appeared from nowhere. A message seemed to have been going on ahead of us: 'Jesus is coming – the one they call the Christ.' By the time we were nearing the city, there was a massive throng around us.

I realise now that the whole afternoon had been planned with great care. People tend to think that, as the twelve disciples, we knew all the details and did everything. It wasn't true. There were plenty of other followers, men and women, who were involved. And the women, in fact, formed the operational heart of much of the work.

Yet, walking so close beside Jesus that afternoon, we did feel a bit special – celebrities at last. Here was a saviour, as King David had been, and we were his disciples. The eyes of the nation were upon us… and it should have been great. Well, I think it was for someone like Peter. He was just drinking it all in. Me? I was swept up by the good mood at the beginning but then I began to wonder where it was all taking us.

I knew how secretive the borrowing of the animals had been. No one was to know about this parade until it happened except for those who were essential to the arrangements. I could see why.

When the crowd yelled 'Hosanna in the highest' or 'Blessed is he who comes in the name of the Lord' it would have sounded harmless enough to the Roman authorities. Just another page in the strange religious celebrations of this set of tribes they had conquered.

When they yelled 'God bless the coming kingdom of our father King David', I thought we were getting towards the edge of what the Romans would tolerate. And when some fools started shouting 'Blessed is the King of Israel', we were well over the line. Fortunately, not everything gets heard by the sentries when a large crowd is on its way.

And the donkey helped the impression of harmlessness. You don't ride into war on a beast of burden. You don't attack your enemies with a symbol of peace and service.

Nonetheless, the Pharisees, who had turned up to check what was going on, heard the words clearly enough and warned Jesus to stop the shouting. It was way too late for that. As he told them, 'If you silence the people, the very stones will cry out.'

I had to think for a moment about what he meant. It was as if what was happening was an avalanche which nobody could turn back and nothing could stop. It was only later I thought it sounded like something from the prophet Habakkuk. He knew his scriptures so much better than any of us did.

We plodded up the steep hillside to the city and entered. I swear that I saw a tear in his eye. He loved Jerusalem but he certainly didn't love everything about it.

I wasn't close enough at that moment to hear clearly what he said. James told me later that he had spoken of how he felt so much sorrow that the city couldn't see what was needed for there to be peace. The price of not grasping it would surely be war and destruction. And all because the people didn't recognise the time that God came to save them.

Jesus went, as we knew he would, to the temple. He didn't stay there long; just quietly surveyed the scene. At one or two things, he looked long and hard.

It should have been great to be back at the centre of our faith on this massive wave of approval but I'm pretty sure our master was not feeling that. His brow was furrowed as he surveyed the temple and a shadow seemed to fall over him.

It wasn't hard to guess what he thought as evening fell upon the temple: so much that should be right and beautiful, overgrown by so much that was wrong and ugly. I suppose we all hoped things would improve but it never seemed to materialise.

He didn't say much as we returned to Bethany. I guess he was still thinking about what he'd seen. In choosing to return to the city, he knew he would be walking into a lions' den. However glamorous our entrance might have been that afternoon, it was only a matter of time until the beasts woke up.

## Where to find this in your Bible:

- Matthew 21:1–11
- Mark 11:1–11
- Luke 19:28–40
- John 12:12–16
- Habakkuk 2:11

# Back in Bethany:
## Martha welcomes the walkers

They returned from their walk into Jerusalem in high spirits and covered in dust. I'm used to that by now. Not everything can be tidy and perfect, however much I'd like it to be. We'd been cooking for hours to ensure there was something warm and nourishing when they returned. Mary had been a real help along with Ruth and several others – a real team effort.

I'd thought Mary would demand to join the group on the walk into the city but she shook her head when I offered her the chance. 'Too much noise, too much fuss,' she told me. 'I like it best when he's out of the spotlight.'

Most of the disciples looked fairly exhausted by the time they returned but they were full of reports about the size of the crowds, the look on the Roman soldiers' faces and the way the temple authorities withdrew to watch from the shadows. Was this good news or bad? I couldn't honestly make up my mind.

Jesus went and sat quietly under one of the olive trees at the far end of the lower field. He used to do that when he was tired or needed some time to think and pray.

We'd had plenty of notice that he was coming on this occasion and had been given clear instructions to share this information only with those who needed to know. As we needed somewhere for every one of them to stay, that actually meant much of the village. But it was fine. Everyone had seen what he'd done for Lazarus. He had nothing but loyal friends here.

They'd arrived the day before and, after the usual smiles and welcomes, I looked round in order to count the numbers. It was nearly exactly what I'd anticipated but there was one extra who I didn't recognise.

'Bartimaeus from Jericho,' declared Peter as he introduced me to the newcomer. 'An extraordinary man… and, for that matter, an extraordinarily loud man. If he needs something, you'll always hear, and tonight I'm guessing that what he'd like most is somewhere to sleep.'

Bartimaeus went red and looked down at his feet. When he looked back up, he mumbled that we weren't to worry about him – he was used to looking after himself and coping with whatever came his way.

'Leave it to me,' I told Peter.

'I knew I could rely on you.'

'Everyone relies on me,' I replied with a smile but feeling slightly cross about this assumption that I'd always be the one to fix things. Peter gave me a big smile, as he always did, and bounded away to deal with the next thing on his list. His head was just full of everything that needed to be done. The difference between him and me, though, was that he managed to delegate a fair bit of it.

'Right, Bartimaeus,' I said. 'Let's see if we can get you sorted.'

'If it's not too much bother,' he said quietly.

For someone who'd just been described as *extraordinarily loud* he was creating exactly the opposite impression. I tried to guess where he fitted into the picture. He clearly wasn't wealthy; his clothes had seen better days and his skin was weather-beaten.

'Don't mind, Peter,' he told me. 'I'm used to sleeping under the stars.'

'Let's get this clear,' I said, rather more firmly than I'd intended. 'Any friend of Jesus is a friend of our village. It will be a pleasure to get you fixed up. And, Ezra, who you're about to meet, was actually complaining that I hadn't placed any guests with him. He gets lonely… you will cheer him up for me, won't you?'

An enormous smile spread across his face. 'You have no idea how glorious it is to feel welcomed and actually wanted. I never thought I would ever experience anything like this.'

'So how did you meet Jesus?' I asked. And he told me the story of his life in Jericho as a blind beggar at the gates on the road between the old and new city. It was a good pitch for calling out from but he was also an easy target for abuse.

'And, when Jesus cured your blindness, what happened then?'

He looked slightly puzzled. 'Well, I got straight up, left everything and followed him.'

'Everything?'

'My begging bowl, my cloak, everything… not that I had much.'

I was impressed. 'Amazing! Although leaving the cloak behind may not have been the greatest idea. It gets a lot colder in Jerusalem than it does in Jericho.'

He laughed and scratched his head, 'I guess you're right. Not clever at all, really. But my heart went out to this man who'd healed me and I just came along with him.'

That evening, when we all ate together, I sat down beside Bartimaeus because I wanted to make sure he felt included. I needn't have worried. He was happy simply to be there and to drink it all in.

He turned to me and said, 'This is good, isn't it? All of us together with Jesus to teach us. And to think I've lived to see days like this!'

It was the word 'see' that touched me and the way he said it. We take the most extraordinary things for granted because they've always been there. Bartimaeus knew how precious sight was. So I looked around the room and took it all in, especially my brother Lazarus. Our new guest was right. The world is a remarkable place if only we'd realise it.

### Where to find this in your Bible:

- John 12:1–2
- Mark 10:46–52

# Now or never:
## Bartimaeus explains himself

When the meal had been cleared away and the talking had died down, people began to turn in for the night. Ezra looked in my direction, I nodded and we left for his little cottage.

'Did you enjoy that parade into Jerusalem, then?' he asked me.

I smiled and scratched my head. 'Not sure. It's a bigger city than I'm used to and there was something a bit scary about it. The alleys get packed so tight it's as if you're not going to be able to breathe. Somehow, though, Jesus manages to rise above it.'

'Is that good? Or do you think that makes him a target for his enemies?'

'Probably both.'

'So how did you meet him? And what was your life before that?'

I hesitated for a moment.

'Tell me in the morning,' he suggested. 'Let's sleep now.'

And we did. Well, Ezra did. I just lay there going over what my life had been like – sat there on the main Jericho road begging for small change from people who were pretending not to see or hear you.

It's not exactly a great life but there are actually worse things in the world than having to beg. It was a good pitch. If you don't mind getting kicked or spat on from time to time, you can make a fair living. I never went hungry. On the other hand, I did grow to hate myself.

That's hard to explain. Farm labourers can have a far worse time than a blind beggar. If the casual work dries up, they have nothing. At least our religion places a duty upon the faithful to give to the poor. That's why the traditional cry to passers-by is 'Give to God'. It's called taking the moral high ground. You could argue that we are actually providing a service!

The trouble was that I wanted to feel I was doing something for the money. I hated the thought that it was a handout, which was made worse by the fact that I'd not always been blind. In fact, I could still see filmy grey shapes but no more than that. My hearing, on the other hand, was fine and I heard the commotion long before the crowd arrived on the day that changed everything.

Guessing there was some celebrity rabbi on his way to Jerusalem for the Passover was easy enough. I asked the crowd who this one was. 'Jesus of Nazareth!', someone yelled across to me.

I knew quite a bit about the teacher from Galilee. As I said, there's nothing wrong with my hearing. He had a curious reputation for being able to do the impossible. I wasn't sure I believed the stories I'd been told but you learned to hold on to the slightest hope in my line of work. Being well-known, I reasoned that at least he might want to show his generosity to my begging bowl. And, if he did, others would inevitably follow.

First, though, I had to grab his attention. I reckoned I'd only have the one chance. At what I calculated was the right moment, I filled my lungs and bellowed, 'Jesus, son of David, have mercy on me.'

It was a bit of a nerve calling him by his family name when we'd never met before, but I wanted him to realise I knew who he was even if he didn't know who I was.

The crowd turned on me. They were listening to what the teacher had to say and wanted to shut me up, but that only made me yell even louder.

I was expecting to get manhandled and roughed up a bit but suddenly it went quiet as if the crowd had stopped moving.

'Cheer up,' said a voice I recognised as someone who used to put money in my bowl. 'He wants to see you.'

I got to my feet and shuffled over. All my confidence had drained away now I was going to meet the man.

'What do you want me to do for you?' he asked.

It sounds like a stupid question but it isn't at all. I'd been shouting for attention and money. If I asked him to 'Give to God' like all the others, I was sure he would. But they said he was a healer. If I asked to see, I would lose my living as a beggar and frankly I had no trade.

At that moment, my mind turned to what my mum looked like when I was little and before my sight started fading. I knew what she would want.

'Master,' I said, very quietly, 'I want to see.'

'Then receive your sight,' he told me. 'You faith has healed you.'

I'd never thought of faith as simply asking for something, but I suppose it is. Somehow, when I was standing by him, I never had any doubt he could do it. The first sight I saw was Jesus himself.

He was smiling at me. I just smiled back. I couldn't think of any words at all. Looking around, I saw my begging bowl and my cloak. As I stood there, Jesus and the crowd began to move forward once more.

Afterwards, people said I'd made a choice there and then. But it didn't seem to me that there was any other thing I could possibly do. If Jesus was heading to Jerusalem, then so was I.

That's what I decided to tell Ezra over breakfast – much the same story as I told Martha when we got to Bethany and she said, 'Let's see if we can get you sorted.' What she can't have known was that those were the exact words my mum would use when I was growing up.

I might have no trade and no obvious means of making a living but I had new friends and I felt safe in a way that I hadn't since I was a young child. Even when you don't know where the road leads, sometimes you simply have to follow it. And, with that thought in my head, I fell sound asleep at last.

### Where to find this story in your Bible?

- Mark 10:46–52
- Luke 18:35–43

# MONDAY

# Miracles are never enough:
## Mary of Bethany worries

The morning after the great parade dawned clear but a little chillier than it had been in the last week. I set about getting organised to make the bread while Martha was dealing with the fire. As I worked, I wondered what the new day would bring.

After the march into Jerusalem yesterday, I'd heard they were planning to return to the temple. Actually, I'm not supposed to call it a march. 'We're not another army out on manoeuvres,' Matthew had insisted when the arrangements for today were being discussed. 'This is about celebrating a new way of doing things; it's a new chapter in our nation's history with the one who is going to make it happen.'

I'm not sure what Jesus would have made of that explanation. It all sounded a bit grandiose and risky to me. I don't like anything which feels like a showdown.

There had been talk for weeks that Jesus was coming up to celebrate the Passover Festival in Jerusalem. The rumours had been circulating for so long that people had begun to think he wasn't coming after all. It didn't stop the Pharisees sending out an order that if anyone spotted him, they were bound by law to report it. That, in their view, guaranteed his arrest.

I'd told Jesus on the evening he arrived that it was no good trying to sneak into the city because someone would spot him and sell their information. He'd smiled.

'It isn't going to work quite like that,' he told me.

On reflection, the plan to ride into Jerusalem did have a touch of utter genius about it. If you can't slip in quietly and privately, make sure you have the biggest crowd imaginable to protect you. If he'd come in surrounded by a Roman legion, he couldn't have been any safer. There was simply no way the Jewish leaders could have touched him on that Sunday.

The only trouble was that he'd laid down a challenge to them. That was never a good idea if you valued your safety. And what he'd done could easily have been construed by the Romans as a threat to them as well. If the Jewish and the Roman authorities got together, he could find himself in very deep water.

I wasn't only worried for Jesus either. The story on everyone's lips was about how he had brought our brother Lazarus back from the dead. If they were going to get rid of Jesus, the word on the street was that they needed to get rid of Lazarus at the same time. But, for one day at least, the authorities seemed powerless.

'Where do you think this is all going to end?' I asked Martha as we started baking.

She furrowed her brow. 'I'm not sure. All I know is that our brother was dead and is alive; that Bartimaeus was blind and now he can see.'

'But will miracles be enough?'

'Miracles are never enough. It's the message by which a faith rises or falls just as it's friendships by which we make our life worth living.'

I gave her an enormous hug. My big sister always seemed to have a wise word or a good plan. I was the dreamer and the worrier. As we worked, I asked her about Bartimaeus.

'He's settling in. I think he's going to stay behind this morning to help Ezra. Said he liked to make himself useful.'

'He seems like a good man.'

'I think he is, and he feels the need to make the most of the return of his sight. I'm not sure he's the most practical of human beings, mind you.'

'But a sweet soul?'

'Absolutely... although I felt a need to mother him a bit. He looked rather overwhelmed by the welcome he had. I just hope it all works out for him.'

'And for us,' I added.

Yes,' she nodded, 'and for us.'

## Where to find this story in your Bible?

- John 11:55–57
- John 12:9–11

# The storm begins:
## Simon Zealot sees tables turned

Breakfast in Bethany is always a good time because you know you're among friends. Even better, friends who bake good bread. On that Monday morning, there was the added bonus of thinking we might be at the beginning of something earth-shattering.

The support we'd experienced as Jesus rode into Jerusalem the previous day was far greater than I had ever expected to see. It seemed to me that, if it all came to a head, the fight might not be won by the old guard. The temple authorities could actually find they didn't have authority anymore. With that thought in my head, every nerve in my body seemed to be strung out on the excitement of it all.

Of course, people had said these things before. I'd seen rebellion come to nothing. When the procession had reached the city yesterday, the weapons of my master's enemies were well-sheathed. Today it might be a different matter. But you could hope. And, on that morning, I did.

We all understood that Jesus would want to return to the temple to give his teaching the widest possible audience in this holiday period. And that was our destination the moment breakfast was finished. However the teaching wasn't what everyone was talking about by the end of the day.

Instead, it was the incident that occurred when we were in the Court of the Gentiles. This outer part of the temple is where everyone can come – male, female, Jew, Greek, anyone from anywhere.

That ought to have made it a magnificent melting-pot. It wasn't. The only part of the whole place where men and women, Jews and non-Jews could pray together had become a seedy and crooked marketplace.

The way that ordinary folk paid their annual gift for the temple should have been simple. But even that involved currency exchange booths as if you were moving into a foreign country, which meant a nice slice of profit for the money-changers. The commission added up to about an extra half day's wages… from every single person.

And that wasn't the worst of it. If you wanted to sacrifice a pair of doves, you needed to buy them in this temple courtyard. And a pair of doves could cost twenty times as much inside the temple than they did outside. Is that fair trading? No, it's daylight robbery. The building at the heart of our faith had become a place where the power was wielded for the benefit of the already powerful.

In spite of that, people had got used to the corruption. Even the High Priest had stalls to fleece the tourists in this bizarre festival marketplace. The hard-nosed would shrug their shoulders and say, 'Well, every priest has a trader.' It had become the way things were and hardly worthy of comment anymore.

Jesus had just looked at it the night before. That morning, he took action. Without a single word, he strode into the middle of all the money-making and starting over-turning tables and benches. It was chaos. Nobody had expected such an action so absolutely no one stopped him.

Some people, as usual, were using the temple as a short cut to get across the city – he stopped that as well, sent people back the way they had come.

Then he turned to those who were staring wide-eyed at what had happened and said, 'Have you ever read your scriptures? Well, have you? It says: "My house will be a house of prayer – for all nations." But what's happened? You have turned the place into a hide-out for crooks and thieves.'

And that was that. He turned away from the mess and started healing people. It was almost more astonishing than the showdown with the traders. He didn't stay angry but went back to doing what he'd always done – looking after people and finding the right words to help them.

The authorities were furious. The Pharisees tried to get him to quieten down his followers. They got nowhere, of course. But I heard them muttering about how this needed to be stopped.

'Good or bad day?' I asked Judas later in a quiet moment. I couldn't make up my mind.

'Good one if he carries it through – they're on the back foot now, however much they may splutter and make their empty threats.'

Then he paused and furrowed his brow. 'But it's a seriously bad day if he backs off having come this far.'

I knew what he meant: the man we had followed was on a knife edge and things could finish up in a dozen different ways. What I didn't guess, even for a moment, was the part Judas Iscariot would play in that.

## Where to find this story in your Bible?

- Mark 11:15–18
- Matthew 21:12–16

# Slipping away:
## Andrew on Monday afternoon

When you look back at troubles, you ask yourself what went wrong. Well, I do, anyway. You think about how it could have been different; you ask why things didn't work out as you had hoped.

Most people I know think the tide turned on that Monday when Jesus threw over the tables in the outer courtyard of the temple. It was the one thing everybody talked about all week and it's true that was the moment when the leaders marked him out as a troublemaker who they needed to eliminate.

Their problem, though, was that they didn't have the power to do much. If you clear out the most corrupt corner of Jerusalem with several sweeps of your hand, you make far more friends than enemies. Friends who will protect you come what may because they believe this is the start of the changes that their land has waited centuries to see.

That afternoon, the crowds were enormous. Not since he'd had to preach from Peter's boat had we seen such a crowd. He looked even more secure in what he was doing than when we arrived the day before in the big parade. People wanted to hear what he had to say, wanted to know what the next step was.

Phillip came across to me with a request from a group of Greek visitors to have some time with Jesus. Like Peter and me, he came from Bethsaida so his spoken Greek was fluent.

The answer I got from Jesus to this puzzled me. It wasn't really an answer at all. Instead he told all who were listening that the hour had come.

For a moment I thought he was talking about our Greek visitors. I was wrong. He talked about his glory, about love and hate, life and death. I wondered whether there was going to be some sort of battle. I wasn't sure.

In fact, there was a whole lot I didn't quite understand and I'm certain I wasn't the only one. He talked about us needing to be ready at a moment's notice and how he was feeling shaken by it all.

Then there seemed to be this voice out of nowhere. I'm convinced I heard the word 'glorified' but others just said it was the sound of thunder. There was no agreement. Sometimes people seem to hear just what they want to hear.

Jesus talked about a world in crisis and the son of man being lifted up. It sounded more like the end of the world to me than a new chapter for Jerusalem.

Other things made perfect sense. When you have the light, you must believe in it and use it, he told us. Then it will be part of you and can shine through every single thing you do. That's us, I thought to myself. He's talking about his followers.

Soon afterwards, we left the city and made our way back to Bethany. As we walked, I tried to make sense of it all.

There were plenty who believed in Jesus, even among the leaders. Mind you, those ones were clearly under serious pressure to keep quiet. Other people didn't seem to get it. I sensed there were already some who were slipping away from him because he didn't say quite what they wanted to hear.

Earlier in the afternoon, he'd told the story of a grain of wheat. He'd had one in his hand. Just a single grain, he'd observed, but if you bury it in the ground it will start growing and produce so much more.

I get that. Sometimes you have to give up what you're doing in order to create something bigger.

On the way back to Bethany, I wondered if Jesus was talking about what he might have to give up. That definitely wasn't what any of us wanted to hear. It was one of those days when I felt I couldn't be certain about anything.

## Where to find this story in your Bible?

- John 12:20–50
- Mark 11:15–18

# Finding the weakness:
## Caiaphas considers a problem

We knew he was coming. As Chief Priest, it's my job to keep a sharp eye on such things. And we knew he'd be trouble. That's why we'd given orders that if anyone knew where he was they were to report it. Not that anyone did. His followers are a clannish bunch; they know how to keep secrets.

When he didn't arrive quite as soon as some people had expected, the gossip turned to how late he might leave it. Then, a bit after that, the chatter suggested he might not be coming at all. I never doubted that he'd turn up and that was why it was important to arrest him before things got out of hand.

The last thing you want when the city is full to bursting is the threat of disorder. And that's exactly what this Galilean preacher represented... especially since stories had started to circulate about Lazarus of Bethany being raised from the dead by him.

That so-called event underlined the problem. He had moved on from just being a rabbi who could explain our faith clearly to visitors and seekers. Now he was someone around whom the discontents of our nation might gather. If he criticised the establishment, it wouldn't be long before boiling point was reached.

I have spent a lifetime shielding us all from the consequences of unsettling our relationship with the Roman authorities and this was sadly just one more chapter in my never-ending work.

Our plan was simple. Arrest the man the moment he appeared. We had several charges in mind but that wasn't what really mattered. Once he was under lock and key, he could stay there until all the noise of the festival had subsided and our visitors had left.

If it became necessary, I believed I could call on my relationship with Pilate to achieve a more permanent solution. I'd told my colleagues in the plainest language that it is better for one man to die for the people than for a whole nation to be destroyed. The statement created an uncomfortable pause but no one argued with me. The potential numbers in such a death count speak for themselves.

I hadn't kept the fact we wanted to arrest him as a secret on the basis that, if he heard, it might put him off coming. As I said, I always doubted that. He wasn't one to be easily discouraged. In fact, I've rarely met anyone stronger in their beliefs. We assumed that he'd try to enter Jerusalem quietly and secretly. On that basis, all we had to do was to stay alert.

What happened was the opposite of what we expected: he arrived in the most public way possible. Like a conquering king but in the trappings of a peacemaker. I have never been so wrong-footed in my whole life.

If we'd arrested him then, I realised that Pilate would hold me responsible for any riot that ensued rather than blaming Jesus himself. I value my position far too much to lose it for the arrest of a provincial preacher.

In such a situation, I did what I've always done: I waited. If he was just engaging in fairly traditional Rabbinic teaching in the temple, I could bear it even if I didn't necessarily like it.

That plan lasted as long as it took him on Monday morning to overturn the tables of the temple traders. This was the challenge to authority that I'd always feared. The trouble was that it brought him an element of public support as well. I didn't believe the other stuff reported to me about healings and heavenly voices but it told me how fevered the atmosphere was.

The council met that evening and we considered our options. There did not seem to be very many of them. All we could agree was that we would seek to unsettle his campaign by drawing him into saying things that would undermine the support he'd been able to gather.

Crowds are fickle. They generally only remember the last thing you've said. And, if those words disappointed or annoyed them, your position was seriously weakened. I can't say it was the strongest plan we'd ever come up with. But when you've got no better idea, you try it.

## Where to find this story in your Bible?

- John 11:45–57
- Mark 11:15–18
- Matthew 21:12–16

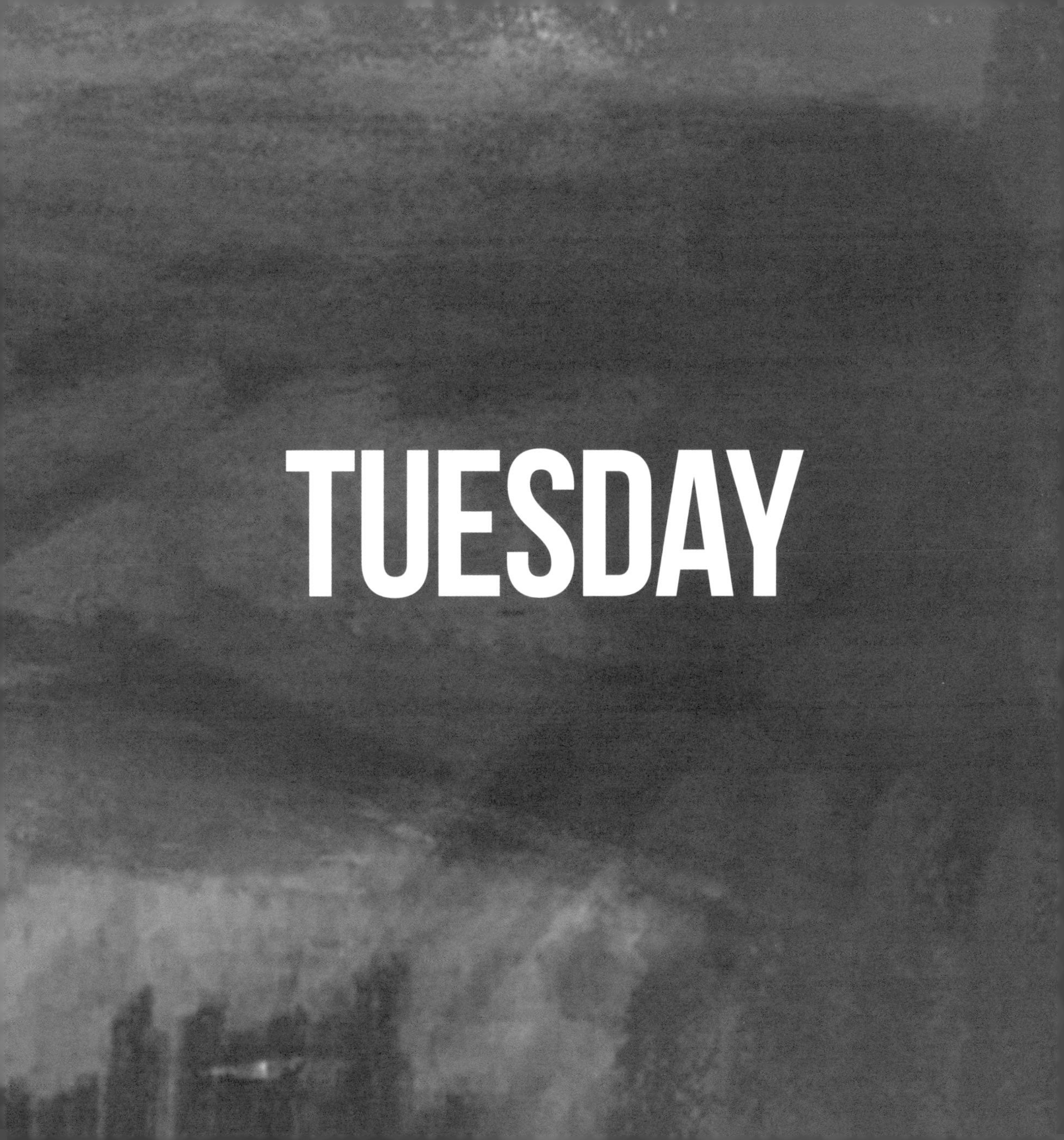

# TUESDAY

# Who really matters:
## Bartimaeus in the cut and thrust

On Tuesday morning, I found myself with Jesus, Mary, the twelve disciples and several others on the road to Jerusalem again. It had felt like a tight-packed, tough, unremitting place on the earlier visit. To be honest, I'd have been quite content to stay behind in Bethany and get on with stuff, but Andrew was insistent. He said that a lad called John Mark wanted to meet me. He'd heard about my story and wanted to see me in person.

'You wouldn't want to disappoint the young lad, would you?' Andrew pointed out.

Put like that, how could I refuse? Mary was with us because she had a message to take from Martha to Joanna. I also suspect she didn't want to miss another opportunity to listen to Jesus. There was a feeling in the air that we didn't quite know how much time there was.

Mary and I walked together that morning, both of us a little anxious but pleased to be included. We talked about ordinary things: baking bread, feeling cold in the morning, what makes a good friend.

Jesus was saying something about faith being able to move mountains and I thought to myself I'm just grateful to be able to move anything. Then he spoke about praying for something and it actually happening. I supposed the day I asked him to let me see was a prayer of sorts so I knew what he meant.

He talked about forgiving as well. The people who had ignored me when I begged at the gate in Jericho came to mind. 'Don't hold grudges,' I told myself.

When we got to the temple courts, a crowd gathered around Jesus and he began teaching them. I didn't hear it all because, after a while, Andrew took me around to meet John Mark. His mother turned out to be the Mary who owned the house with the large upper room where the disciples sometimes met.

The part Jesus said that day which I did hear made me feel the clouds were gathering. After a while, the ordinary listeners were obliged to make space for the temple leaders: the priests, the teachers, the elders. They gave an unmistakeable impression that they were in charge. 'What's your authority for all this?' they demanded of Jesus.

Well, they would ask that, wouldn't they? The bosses never like their noses being put out of joint. But I think it was probably a trick too: a way of getting him to say something that was blasphemous so they could deal with him.

Jesus replied that he'd tell them what his authority was, if they'd tell him where John the Baptist's authority came from.

That was tricky for them. They'd ignored John when he was here even though almost everyone felt his words came from God himself. So they claimed that they really didn't quite know about John.

Jesus smiled and told them that if they couldn't even decide on that, he wasn't going to explain where his authority came from. Fair enough. And, to be honest, you didn't need to ask about his authority because everyone could sense it. There was a power to his words that could only come from beyond this world.

So instead of explaining what gave him a right to speak as he did, he told the story of two sons who were asked by their dad to help out in the vineyard. The first told him that he didn't want to but changed his mind and turned up anyway. The second one said, 'certainly father, I'll be happy to help' and then conveniently forgot all about it.

Immediately, I was thinking of families where that happened all the time and of the polite people who never actually got down to any real work. But that wasn't why he told the story. He was thinking of John the Baptist and how the rogues and crooks changed their behaviour when they came to the Jordan while the Jewish leaders kept their distance and did nothing different at all.

Then he told a story about a man who had hired out his fabulous vineyard to people who he believed would be reliable. Not a good choice. When he sent for his share of the profits, the people he had trusted turned on the owner's servants, beat them and killed them. Even when his son was sent, he met the same fate. It sounded like the story of all God's prophets across the centuries with the Jewish people.

He finished by reminding them of a psalm – 'The stone which the builders rejected as worthless has become the most important one of all.'

It was when he said those words that the penny dropped properly – he was the one the establishment was turning against. For all our differences, I suddenly realised he knew how I felt as I begged by the gate because the rejection was happening to him as well. But that's not the most important bit for anyone who's ever felt on the outside of things. He was pointing out that the rejected ones, whatever some people may think, can become the most important ones of all.

### Where to find this story in your Bible?

- Matthew 21:21–42
- Mark 11:22—12:10
- Luke 20:1–17

# The trap:
## Matthew on the money

When Bartimaeus was leaving with Andrew to meet up with John Mark, I leaned across and said quietly, 'Don't bring the young lad to the temple this afternoon. I've a feeling this could become nasty.'

I didn't say it but I'd heard the muttered threats of some of our so-called leaders. It amazed me how they could strut around looking so religious while a whole cesspit of evil ideas bubbled away just below the surface.

The cliques who run our city were talking in whispers to each other about putting him away. I thought to myself: if they do it now, they'll spark the biggest riot in living memory.

While they stood there, going over in their heads what they could and couldn't do, Jesus told a story of a king who had prepared a grand wedding feast. Those who had been officially invited made all sorts of excuses not to attend. Eventually the wedding went ahead simply with the people who could be found in the neighbourhood, good and bad.

I was half-listening to Jesus and half-watching the Jewish leaders. It was another story about the establishment being side-lined while anyone and everyone took their place. Those who are chosen, he seemed to be saying, are unlikely to be any of the folk you call your leaders.

Small wonder they wanted to arrest him. The problem was how… and their answer to that turned out to be a question about money. It's always a good subject to get people taking sides and then disagreeing with each other. The plan included a curious combination of people. The Pharisees turned up with a small group of Herodians, the only Jews who ever seemed to be sympathetic to the Romans.

'What are they doing together?' I wondered. They were not exactly regular bedfellows. The answer, I guessed, must involve something of interest not only to the Jewish nation but to Rome as well. Still, I honestly didn't see the specific question coming.

'Teacher,' the Pharisees said to Jesus, 'we know you are an honest man and don't say things just to please people. So tell us, frankly: is it right to pay taxes to Caesar or not?'

My mouth dropped open. If anyone understood the great pit that they'd opened up in front of my master it was me. I'd collected those taxes for long enough and been spat upon for my work more often than not. For a minute, I was back at my counting table feeling the loathing of all the folk paying what the Emperor required of them.

Jesus was cornered whatever his answer. If he said it was right to pay taxes to Caesar, he would appear to be putting the Roman Emperor before God himself and his support would begin to evaporate. If he said people shouldn't pay taxes to Caesar, he would be arrested and could quite possibly face the death penalty.

Jesus turned to face his enemies. 'You're playing games,' he told them with genuine anger. 'Bring me a coin.'

They were puzzled but gave him a denarius.

'There,' he said. 'Who is that on the coin? Whose name is there?'

'Caesar,' they replied.

'Well,' said Jesus, handing back the coin, 'give to Caesar what belongs to Caesar and make sure you give to God what is his.'

The Pharisees were speechless. Well, you would be, wouldn't you? Even an ex-tax-collector like myself couldn't have fashioned an answer anywhere near as good as that. But I wondered how often these unexpected twists in the story could continue before he was left with no more words that could make a difference.

### Where to find this story in your Bible?

- Matthew 21:45; 22:1–22
- Mark 12:13–17
- Luke 20:20–26

# Men with an agenda:
## Mary of Bethany hears the questions

I delivered Martha's message to Joanna and we agreed we'd go together to hear Jesus in the temple's outer court. The Herodians were there when we arrived.

Joanna smiled quizzically. 'A few faces I recognise here,' she observed, 'but no one that I'd expect to be a fan of the man from Nazareth.'

We soon found out what was up – a trap to put Jesus in trouble with his followers or in prison under Roman guard. It didn't work. His answer about Caesar, money and God wrong-footed all of them.

I settled down to hear whatever came next, pleased that Martha had found me a task that earned me time to listen to my Lord. Joanna stayed by me and gave my hand a little squeeze. I knew what that meant. She was grateful to be with friends for a while rather than in the cut and thrust of Herod's court.

A couple of Sadducees were the next to ask a question. Well, it was a bit more than a question actually. It was a thoroughly complicated rigmarole about one woman and far too many men which didn't make any sense in my eyes. The reason for the story was simple enough: they believed that once you're dead, you're dead, full stop. No argument.

In their made-up tale there were seven brothers. The woman married the first and he promptly died without her having any children. As the law of Moses directed, the second brother married the woman but then he… I could see where this was going: seven brothers marrying one woman and not a single sign of a son or daughter anywhere. However we all had to wait while they wound their way through the whole silly story.

The question, if you can call it that, was who would the woman be married to in the afterlife. It was their way of arguing against resurrection, heaven, anything after death.

I can't be sure, but I'm almost certain I heard Jesus give a quiet sigh when they had finally finished. You could hardly blame him if he did. I wondered how often he had put up with nonsense like this.

'Look and think,' Jesus told those who had asked the question. 'Look at our scriptures and think about our God. Marriage is for this time not for all the times to come. Think of yourself in the next world as all being God's children, like the angels. As for your idea of the dead not rising, what did God say to Moses? He said "I am the God of Abraham." God isn't talking about someone in the past here, he's obviously talking about the living.'

'That's a great answer,' said one of the teachers who was there and others agreed with him. Not the Sadducees, of course. They huddled in the corner and muttered. In fact, no one came forward with any more clever debating points after that. I think they were actually a little scared of him.

However, one of those who had been impressed by Jesus did bring up a matter about the law. 'Which of all our rules is the most important?' he asked. Now that's a proper question. Instead of men with an agenda we had a genuine enquiry. That's because it came from someone who hadn't already decided what the answer should be.

'Most important?' Jesus mused. 'Well, there is one God so love him with all your heart, with all your soul, with all your mind, with all your strength.'

I thought to myself: that just about includes every part of us, every single thing we think and say and do.

'There's another rule that goes with the first one,' Jesus added, 'Love your neighbour just as much as yourself.'

The teacher raised his eyebrows and smiled. 'One God to love and serve with all our might! That is so right and much more powerful than any worship and sacrifice we can perform here.' You could see that Jesus had warmed to the man. I suppose he felt he had been understood at last.

Jesus told him, 'You are not far from the kingdom of God itself.'

And, suddenly, I could see how right Martha had been to send me out that morning. The day was a treat, a blessing. I've always enjoyed listening to Jesus and this time I also saw what his answers meant for me. It was absolutely right to listen, to feel, to understand. But you are not truly whole unless you act on what you discover.

## Where to find this story in your Bible?

- Matthew 22:23–40
- Mark 12:18–34
- Luke 20:27–40

# Prayer night:
## John keeping watch

Returning from the temple to Bethany never felt better than it did that Tuesday evening. Back in the countryside none of us had to worry about what we said or who might be listening to us. It was a place where Jesus could be himself and so could we.

After supper, our master left the village to spend time on the Mount of Olives. There was an olive grove which belonged to a friend of our movement: a quiet place where he used to pray, think and, on warm spring nights, sleep quietly under the stars.

I sensed he would have been happy to have been there alone but, in that last week, at least some of us were nearly always with him. We didn't trust the priests or the council or Herod or Pilate. Any of them might want to see Jesus out of the way. In fact, he may have chosen to take his rest beyond the village itself in order to avoid an incident that would put Lazarus or any of the others at risk.

On Tuesday, Simon Zealot said he'd join him. He didn't ask, just stated it and Jesus didn't refuse. I asked to join them too and they both nodded. Often, I do things with Simon Peter and my brother James, but I also get on with the other Simon. His unwavering passion for a faith that wouldn't lie down and be compromised was exhilarating and made him a formidable opponent if an enemy was in view.

That night he had his sword with him as usual but a weapon wasn't needed. We had the mountainside to ourselves and stayed quietly in the shadows as our master prayed.

Sometimes he did so silently but other parts we heard clearly enough. The words 'why' and 'how' came up more than once. That was no surprise. Why on earth were people trying to catch him out? Why couldn't they see what we could see? And how could all this be changed? Even if we didn't catch everything that he was saying, we sensed where his prayers led.

It felt like he was sifting through what was left for him to say and do. This was about his next moves, and I guess, looking back at it now, how many moves were left.

Simon Zealot had always believed that passion for the faith would win through and that people would eventually be swept up in a wave of nationalism which even the Romans couldn't deny. It was a wonderful way to look at the world but the trickery I'd watched play out in the temple itself had almost convinced me it was never going to happen.

The trouble I saw on our master's face that evening made me feel I was right to be pessimistic. Yet, for all the doubts and concerns, there was a moment when the lines on my Lord's face relaxed and he looked hopeful again. 'Thank you,' I heard him whisper, 'for the one who asked and understood what love is all about. He is not far from us, is he? I am grateful for that.'

It occurred to me, after he had said those words, that one person who reaches out can sometimes make all the difference, not just to us but to Jesus too.

## Where to find this story in your Bible?

- Luke 21:37
- Mark 12:28–34

# WEDNESDAY

# A different question:
## Simon Peter on the end of the debate

'I hope it isn't going to be like yesterday,' I told John as we took the road into Jerusalem on Wednesday morning. Tuesday had seemed to me like a day of everyone trying to catch Jesus out. People, one after another, seemed to have been trying to get him to say something that compromised him. The authorities were simply desperate to make Jesus look dangerous or stupid… or both.

John told me a little bit about what he'd heard the previous evening as Jesus prayed. It sounded to me as if, at heart, Jesus was asking the same question I always seem to, 'What do I do next?'

Actually, if it had been me praying, it would have been, 'How do I avoid tomorrow being like the day before?' When we got to the temple, I expected not much more than a repeat of Tuesday but it didn't happen. This time, Jesus himself started off with a question.

'Tell me,' he asked the Pharisees as soon as they had spotted and cornered him, 'what do you think about the one who is to come, the one you call the Christ, the Messiah? Whose son will he be?'

It sounded a lot less tricky than 'Should we pay taxes to Caesar or not?'

The leader of the group turned to Jesus and said, 'The Son of David.'

His tone implied that our master was a fool to ask a question as basic as that.

I smiled to myself. Of course I didn't know exactly what was coming but I guessed something was.

'If you're right,' Jesus continued, 'why does David himself call the one who is to come *Lord* when he's swept up in God's Spirit as he writes the Psalms?'

Then he quoted the opening line of number 110 which even the most half-hearted members of our faith know because it talks of the Messiah who will change everything.

It's the very first words of that psalm which most people remember: 'The Lord said to my lord.' Jesus was right: David called the Christ figure 'Lord' all those centuries ago.

I could see what was surely coming next. It would be a version of the question he asked us when we were in Caesarea Philippi: 'Who do you say that I am?'

Perhaps they sensed that, because they gave him no answer at all. Instead, they withdrew. It was the last time there was any debating. And I felt that was a tragedy, at least for them.

This was their chance to listen and to think about what sort of a leader they had been looking for. David was a great man, a brilliant military strategist, at least in his youth. His knowledge of warfare kept him alive when others wanted him dead and the power of his presence united the nation.

Yet it hadn't been enough. Things fall apart when you least expect them to. I was certain of the very thing the Pharisees feared – that Jesus was indeed the Messiah. The one who was to come had actually arrived.

But, as in David's time, I sensed that power and strategy might not be enough. However much I hated hearing Jesus talk about suffering and service, I was beginning to sense they might be things we had to go through – the darkness that leads to the light.

I didn't like the thought in the slightest. As for the Pharisees, they weren't even ready to consider anything like that.

## Where to find this story in your Bible?

- Matthew 22:41–46
- Mark 12:35a–37
- Luke 20:41–44

# Hitting hard:
## Matthew listening in the temple

When the Pharisees withdrew on Wednesday morning, they left Jesus with a massive crowd and I wondered what would happen. I didn't have to wait for long. It was as if the absence of the authorities had released a passion he had held in check.

'There's nothing basically wrong,' he told the crowd, 'with what the teachers are teaching – it's what Moses told our people back at the start. The problem is what they're doing with it. They package up what Moses said in a way that makes it a massive load for every one of you to carry.

'And as for your leaders' lives: look at them. You'll see one instance of showing-off after another – the best seats at the feasts, the finest-looking clothes and the desire to be seen so that everyone can greet them with respect. They just love it!

'If you really want to stand out, you must be a servant to everyone else. Whoever sees themselves as important is heading for a fall. Whoever reckons they deserve hardly anything will find they receive far more than they ever imagined.'

Listening to this, I thought it was a good job the Pharisees and the teachers of the law had left. Otherwise my master would have been in even deeper water than before. What I didn't realise was that he'd only just begun.

'Hypocrites!' he declared. 'That's what these people are. All their behaviour achieves is to lock the door to heaven. Not just for them but for those who follow them. Blind guides!'

He talked more then about how complicated they make the rules and how much they love the detail. Not the rules that Moses gave but the detail they've made up and added in so they can seem holier than the rest of us. They know how to be strict and exact in their giving, he explained, but then don't have the generosity of heart to fill the world with fairness, faithfulness and mercy.

By the time he'd finished, a 'blind guide' was definitely not the only thing he called our leaders. 'Whitewashed tombs' was the phrase that hit home with me – getting the outside looking neat and tidy while what the place actually contained was decaying bones and rotting corpses.

It was hard-hitting stuff, yet it was a fair comment. Jerusalem had always been a place where the prophets were ignored at best and killed all too often. That Jesus loved the city was never in doubt. It made his declaration that one day everything would come crashing down even more tragic.

As for my master's future, I shuddered as I listened to him. The ordinary people might like what he was saying but with our leaders he'd be even less popular than I'd been as a tax collector. Being spat upon is bad enough. I knew that. But he was risking something a whole lot worse.

When he'd finished, we moved across to where the offerings were made: a quiet moment at last. The rich people were doing just what Jesus had been talking about: making a show of their giving and their virtue.

I thought to myself how much some people like to be in the spotlight, although I wondered if I was actually so different. Then Jesus pointed out an elderly widow. I'd never have spotted her as she slipped in and out very quickly to place a couple of copper coins into the great treasury chest. It amounted to next to nothing financially.

'Think about what she's done,' he told us. 'The rich can easily afford what they've given. That's all she has. In truth, she's actually given more than any of the others.'

For an ex-taxman, it was a sobering moment. I'd always concentrated on what I was getting so the books balanced. It had never occurred to me to think about what people were giving me. Being with Jesus didn't turn my world upside down just once. Somehow he managed to do it again and again.

## Where to find this story in your Bible?

- Matthew 23:1–39
- Mark 12:37b–44
- Luke 20:45–47; 21:1–4

# Dark days ahead:
## Simon Peter walking back to Bethany

There's something unnervingly temporary about time. Once it's gone, it's over, full stop.

Before we had started out on the road to Jerusalem, I'd got Jesus on his own and told him what I thought about the dangers of a showdown with the authorities. He'd set out the risks clearly enough in talking to us yet still seemed determined to take them. Basically, I told him it was foolish.

'You talk like men do,' he told me. 'You don't think like God does.'

Suddenly, I found I'd crossed the line between good and evil in his eyes. He was right; I was trying to avoid the hard parts of life and however much I wished I hadn't said what I had, it was done.

The moment passed, as time does, but it left its imprint.

And now we were leaving Jerusalem on the day before the Passover Supper after the most explicit and fierce attack he'd ever made on the leaders of the nation. Things felt as if they were coming to a head, and I didn't like it any more now than when he'd first talked about returning to the city.

As we came out beyond the walls of Jerusalem, one of us – it might have been Phillip – turned and looked back. The sheer size of the stones used to build the temple is incredible and he couldn't help saying how magnificent it looked.

Jesus paused and stared with him at the scene. 'Not a single stone will be left on top of another,' he told us. 'It will all be thrown down. Every single bit of it.'

That stopped the conversation in its track and we walked silently for quite some time. After a while we took a break, as we often did when we'd got well out into the countryside, at his friend's olive grove. For a little while, we felt we had Jesus to ourselves.

What we desperately wanted to know was when this destruction of the temple would take place. Time, you see. Everyone wants to know how long they've got.

He told us about wars and rumours of wars, about those who would claim to be *The One* but weren't anything of the sort. He also warned us about how we'd find ourselves in the line of fire. He explained how we'd suffer in times to come but also how we'd be given the words to speak when the pressure was on us.

It was a dark, dark place he brought to mind where love would grow cold and betrayal could strike from the hands of people you thought most cared for you. All you could do was be on your guard and watch out. There seemed to be no escape from this nightmare world where the sun would be darkened and the stars would fall from the sky. Yet not everything and everyone would be lost.

I wanted to shout 'When?' at him because I wanted to know what time we had left. But I didn't dare. All we got was the promise that this generation would not pass away until all the things he described had happened.

It wasn't the answer I longed for and I desperately wanted to tell him so but the wrong words had come out of my mouth far too many times. Instead I listened as he told us to keep watch because no one knows the time. It was as if he knew what I'd been thinking.

Then: the odd bit. He reminded us about three of his parables. The first concerned young girls getting ready for a wedding, the second involved servants being given money to invest and the third was about separating people like sheep and goats at the end of the age.

It made absolutely no sense to me at the moment he said it, but it does now. His stories normally had one important point to get across and these seemed so different. But they weren't.

The connection came to me as I was drifting off to sleep that evening. The key that unlocks them is time. In each case, the challenge is to use it well. And, whatever I needed to do, it had to be done as if I was doing it for Jesus. At that moment, I had no idea how badly I'd use time in the days to come or how much I'd hate myself for the things I did and didn't do. You might assume that all this talk about dark days ahead would weigh me down as things spiralled out of control but it didn't.

I remembered his words and tried to hang on to the hope that not everything would be lost. I didn't always manage that because sometimes I felt I'd ruined every chance I'd ever had. But, even when I felt so lost that I would never be found again, there was another voice telling me that it only felt like the end. Time was still turning.

## Where to find this story in your Bible?

- Matthew 16:13–23; 24:1–25, 46
- Mark 13:1–37
- Luke 21:5–36

# A quiet safe place:
## Caiaphas plans his move

They had left Jerusalem by the time the council met on that Wednesday; disappeared into the countryside yet again. Not that we didn't have a very good idea where they were likely to be. But Bethany would have been almost as much of a problem as Jerusalem if you wanted to arrest this thorn in our flesh. What we needed was somewhere that the lunatic fringe who followed him wouldn't make it difficult for us.

Actually, the word 'fringe' doesn't do justice to the challenge we were facing. What he'd been saying and doing meant that we were dealing with a whole lot more than a fringe. There were hundreds who would fall in behind him if he decided to rise up against our authority.

The council has invested hours, months and years in order to maintain a modicum of independence in the face of the Roman imperial machinery. It requires tact, compromise and, most of all, it demands that we keep a lid on the hotheads who might undermine our hard-won position.

Part of the problem with Jesus of Nazareth lay in the fact that he wasn't a hothead in the normal sense of the word. He was a classic reformer: the sort that wants the heart and soul of our religion to be transformed and renewed. There were people among the Pharisees and even on our council who felt much of what he said made sense.

That's all very well but this wasn't the time for such matters. The balance of power was delicate and unstable. It was the job of my family to hold things in check so that balance remained. Not easy, I can tell you.

And this provincial preacher threatened to undo all my good work in the space of a few days. From the moment he overturned the tables of the traders in the temple, I knew we'd end up having to deal with him in one way or another. However it was what he had said on Wednesday morning which really drove home to me the seriousness of the matter.

After the Pharisees were so neatly wrong-footed by him on the question of King David and the one who will come to save us, they withdrew. Frankly, I sometimes wished we had the Galilean preacher on our side – he was so much brighter and more incisive than most of the crew I have to work with.

Perhaps he thought that when they were gone he could say what he liked but there's always someone lurking in the shadows to report back to me. I didn't mind his different interpretation of Moses. Rabbis have been doing that for centuries. It was his personal attack on the Pharisees that spelt out the danger.

Between you and me, the word 'hypocrites' is fair comment on some of them but the phrase 'whitewashed tombs' crosses a red line. Mind you, that's not as damaging as 'blind guides'. Someone has to lead the people and keep them safe in this unstable, occupied land of ours. If the Jewish Council starts to be ignored or rejected by people, it will be a short step to chaos and bloodshed. I know how the Romans work even if others choose to ignore it.

I called a meeting for late afternoon to discuss what was to be done. Actually, it was more a matter of how it was to be done. We needed this troublemaking preacher out of the way. The challenge was how we could do it.

We couldn't arrest Jesus in the city. The moment people knew we had done it, there would be massive unrest: exactly the kind of thing we were trying to avoid. Bethany was a slightly better bet but, if there was resistance and someone got killed, the news would filter back to Jerusalem in next to no time with the risk of unrest probably even greater than before.

What we needed was a safe, quiet place where we could take the man without too much resistance. Given what he'd said in his teaching, I suspected he'd come quietly. He'd spent enough time talking about himself as a peacemaker.

There was also the problem of the Passover Festival itself – the arrest would need to be before or after it. Otherwise, we might even have a full-blown rebellion on our hands.

Our meeting solved nothing. But it did come to an agreement that all of us would look at ways and means by which we could do what was necessary. What none us of guessed was how that would actually happen or how close we were to a possible solution.

### Where to find this story in your Bible?

- Matthew 26:1–5
- Mark 14:1–2
- Luke 22:1–2

# Extravagant love:
## Bartimaeus on an unexpected act

The disciples returned from Jerusalem that Wednesday evening in sombre mood. The hard-hitting criticism of the Pharisees had made them nervous. Andrew admitted it had felt as if Jesus was talking about things that sounded like the end of the world.

I'd not joined them because I'd stayed in Bethany to help in the preparations for a special supper with Jesus as the honoured guest. Not the Passover supper – that would be tomorrow – but a sort of 'thank you' to Jesus for all he'd done.

It was at Simon's house and, as usual, Martha was in charge. There's a fine line between caring and domineering but Martha seemed aware of the danger.

'Something Jesus once said,' she told me. 'You have to turn on listening and thinking before you launch into talking and doing. I know I'm not always good at that but I'm working to be better.'

I put my hand on her shoulder, 'From what I'm seeing, you seem to me to be working it out just fine.'

She smiled. 'What makes you special, Bartimaeus, is that you appreciate everyone around you and you actually say so. It makes all the hard work worthwhile.'

And it was hard. But, by the time we sat down together, everything was fine and we seemed set for a quiet evening. It didn't work out quite like that though.

Towards the end of the meal, a woman called Mary took an alabaster jar of perfume, broke open the neck and poured it onto Jesus' head and feet. She must have used the entire jar, the whole house was filled with the aroma of expensive perfume.

Some were astonished; others were embarrassed; one disciple was furious. Judas Iscariot demanded to know why the perfume couldn't have been sold and the money given to the poor. That was worth a full year's wages he declared. A few nodded in agreement.

I could see the point Judas was making. After all, I knew how hard it was to appeal for people's charity. But there was something I didn't like about the way he said it. Was it actually worth a year's wages? That seemed like a bit of an exaggeration to me. I couldn't be sure but I suspect Judas wasn't any more certain of his claim than I was.

It was as if some sort of anger had been bubbling inside of him and had suddenly boiled over. Of course, he was the one charged with looking after the money so he had more reason than most to comment.

Only later did I hear the rumour that he'd looked after himself as much as the disciples when he'd been in charge of the cash. I don't know the truth of that but his reaction seemed as excessive, in its way, as Mary's generosity.

Jesus turned to those who were being so critical. He asked them why they were so angry and told them to leave her alone. It was a beautiful thing that she did, he insisted, because he was not going to be with us much longer.

Then he said something about burial and good news that I didn't quite follow but I'd learnt not to worry about the things I didn't fully understand. Most of life's puzzles slot into place if you give them time.

He also said something that has stayed with me ever since. 'You will always have the poor with you,' he explained, 'but you will not also have me.'

I hated the thought that there might always be poor people. I loathed the idea that, in years to come, someone would have to beg as I had. But I could see his point. Things get better and then a disaster overwhelms a person, a city or even a whole nation. So there will probably always be someone who will need our help in one way or another.

And I would much prefer to meet people who are able to show extravagant love rather than those who only know how to give themselves to others in carefully measured portions.

After the meal was over, I didn't take the opportunity to join the men as they left for evening prayer; I stayed to clear up with Mary and the others. It seemed the right choice to make. Doing so, I spotted Judas peeling off and heading in a different direction from the main group. At that moment, I just assumed he'd been sent on an errand.

## Where to find this story in your Bible?

- Luke 10:38–41
- Matthew 26:6–13
- Mark 14:3–9
- John 12:2–8

# Thirty pieces:
## Caiaphas makes an offer

We'd finished our meal and my fellow leaders were just getting ready to leave for the night when it happened – a knock at the door.

'Who on earth can that be now?' complained Annas. He's getting too old to have patience with any out-of-hours business that comes our way. And it does in this city, believe me.

One of the temple guards who was on duty came in and whispered a message to me.

'Who?' I demanded – not quite believing what I was hearing. 'Well, don't leave him outside. Get the man in here!'

It was Judas, the one called Iscariot. I knew of him because that was the disciple who usually dealt with the temple taxes for Jesus and his group. He was also one of the radicals within the Galilean's raggle-taggle team.

'Welcome,' I said, as he came in looking cautiously from side to side for any suggestion of danger.

'You're quite safe here,' I told him, 'and what you say will stay within these walls.'

It wasn't true of course but I felt the man needed reassurance. He told me he'd had enough, was willing to hand his master over to us. I was not sure I believed him.

'What will you give me if I hand him over?'

'One moment,' I told him and gathered my close colleagues in a corner. They were more than eager to make an offer. We decided to start at thirty pieces of silver.

He took it immediately, rather too hurriedly for my liking. The agreement was that he'd look out for an opportunity to pass Jesus over to us quietly when no crowd was present. Easier said than done I thought, but we were only risking thirty silver pieces on it. In my view, that was cheap… if it worked.

But would it? Were we being lured into a trap? I didn't like it at all but the rest were delighted with the deal we were making. I've been in this work too long to get excited until a problem is finally put to bed.

I looked long and hard at the man with whom we were cutting a deal and I realised I couldn't read him. He was a closed book. Perhaps he had come across to our side and wanted a new chapter in his life. Or perhaps he was up to something I hadn't yet worked out. Only time would tell.

## Where to find this story in your Bible?

- Matthew 26:14–16
- Mark 14:10–11
- Luke 22:3–6

# THURSDAY

# Morning preparations:
## John on a secret mission

I slept slightly longer than usual after the meal the previous evening and was woken by my older brother shaking my shoulder.

'Come on, snoring boy, the rest of us are up. It's Passover supper, tonight.'

'All you ever think about is food,' I told him. 'I could have been lying here quietly praying.'

'But you're not, so get up,' he demanded.

I was secretly glad he'd woken me because I hate the idea that I might miss something. I'm the one in the family who likes to do the detailed stuff.

As it happened, there was at least one detail about the day that none of us knew: the venue for the supper. I'd asked Peter the evening before if he knew. He shook his head.

'Bit strange,' I said.

Peter gave me a look that suggested he was slightly bothered in the same way I was. 'It's not what he usually does but this is a troublesome week in all sorts of ways. I suspect he's deliberately not told us the details.'

'Because we're unreliable?'

Peter laughed briefly, 'We've always been unreliable. He'd have never told us a single thing on that basis. No, I think it's because he doesn't want anyone to hear who might pass messages on about where it's to be.'

That sounded a little bit ridiculous out here in sleepy old Bethany but Jesus did very little, if anything, without good reason. Once we'd gathered together and were eating Martha's fantastic fresh bread, Phillip asked Jesus where he'd like us to make arrangements for the supper that evening.

'It is all in hand,' he told Phillip and then he turned to Peter and me. 'I want you to take our usual route to the city. When you get there, a man carrying a water jar will meet you. You do not have to say anything, just follow him.'

'He will take you to a house where you are to say to its owner – "The teacher asks: where is the guest room where my disciples and I may eat the Passover meal?" You'll be shown a large upper room which should be ready for us. Make our preparations there.'

Peter said, 'A bit of a mystery, like last Sunday's arrangements, then.'

Jesus frowned, 'Only a bit like that.'

We set off straight away. It was a fresh spring morning, the sort on which you can believe all the best things in life are before you. Except that wasn't how we felt on this occasion.

The plan worked without a hitch. A young man was resting in the shade of the city wall just outside the gate. When he saw us drawing near, he nodded almost imperceptibly, lifted a great water jar on to his shoulder and ambled casually through the gate. We followed silently.

I recognised parts of the route we took but it certainly wasn't the quickest way to our destination. At one point we almost lost him in the market bustle but he slowed and the water jar on his shoulder was just enough for us not to lose track.

When we got there, I was puzzled. 'Isn't this where John Mark lives with Mary his mother?' I asked Peter.

He nodded, 'My brother brought Bartimaeus here to meet Mark earlier in the week.'

'So what was the point of complicating it all?'

'In order to be complicated, I think. Could you have followed us through those streets?'

'Probably not,' I admitted.

'Then, probably, we haven't been followed.'

Our guide didn't enter the main part of the house but took us to a set of stairs which led to an upper room. It looked pretty well prepared before we did anything. Mary Magdalene, who had been staying in Jerusalem, was there.

'Welcome,' she said. 'How is everyone?'

'A little edgy,' Peter confessed, 'but then it's been a difficult week. Have you done all this sorting out for us?'

She smiled, 'Mary and I have made a start but you'll doubtless have your own ideas. Just tell me what else you need and I'll sort it. It's easy enough for me to be out on the city streets without any comment. If you make yourselves visible, the information is liable to be with the temple authorities in less than five minutes.'

'It feels like we're hiding from the scene of a crime,' I observed.

Mary Magdalene nodded, 'The only difference may be that we're trying to stop the crime from happening.'

## Where to find this story in your Bible?

- Matthew 26:17–19
- Mark 14:12–16
- Luke 22:7–13

# Feet first:
## Simon Peter on saying too much

We didn't stay long in Jerusalem, an hour or so I would guess, and then left in the same way we entered thanks to our guide. I never discovered his name but I never forgot his help. Without him, that final supper might never have happened.

Our return in the evening occurred only when the sun had set and we could move about with less chance of being observed. Jesus had a look of focused determination on his face. I'd known how much he'd wanted to celebrate this Passover in Jerusalem and I assumed that was what the look meant. Even then, we had little idea what was to happen next.

Once we were safely together in that upper room, Jesus went downstairs briefly to speak with our host family. It gave us a chance for the sort of discussion that often broke out when we had some time to spare.

On this occasion, the subject was which of us might turn out to be the greatest – the sort of silly argument that we should all have grown out of... but hadn't.

Of course, Jesus wasn't in the room as the discussion gathered pace and began to sound like an argument. When he returned, we immediately calmed down. Strangely, he didn't say a word, just went to the end of the room.

There, he took off his outer clothing, wrapped a towel around his waist and poured water into a basin. For once, I could see exactly what was going to happen and I was appalled. He actually started washing our feet and drying them with the towel wrapped around his waist. The other disciples were astonished and speechless.

When he got to me, I had to say something. 'What are you doing washing my feet?' I asked him.

'It may not make sense now,' he told me, 'but one day it will.'

I tried to stop him. 'Never!' I declared. 'You should never have to wash my feet.'

'But I must,' he told me. 'Unless I do this, you cannot be a part of the work I am doing.'

'Then all of me,' I replied, 'hands and head as well,' which was a bit of a jump from never but I'm afraid that's me.

He explained how it wasn't necessary and I get that now. You see, it was like a parable taking place, with us as a part of it. We saw ourselves as his servants but, at some time in the future, liked the idea of being very important in our own right. He wanted us to know it wouldn't be like that. Each one of us had been put here for others, not just for ourselves.

Not only did he stop us in our tracks, we never went back to arguing which one of us would be the biggest and the best. After that night, whenever I began to get ideas too grand for my head to fit through a doorway, I'd close my eyes and see Jesus kneeling at my feet. Then I'd think to myself: *he loved me enough to serve me and to wash my feet.* If he could do something like that, then so could I.

## Where to find this story in your Bible?

- Luke 22:24
- John 13:1–20

# One of us:
## Simon Zealot watches his friend

From time to time, I get asked what it was like to have Jesus wash my feet. Well, it was strange and uncomfortable in a way but it was also very welcome after the walk. Of course it would normally be Mary's servant who would do that task but, for some reason, he wasn't around that evening.

I wasn't shocked like Peter. After all I've seen across the years, nothing surprises me. And everything our master did had a point to it. However, Peter wasn't the only one who looked very uncomfortable about what was happening. My friend Judas looked totally shocked and appalled, although he didn't say anything.

It could have been because he thought it was inappropriate as Peter clearly did but I suspect it went deeper than that. When I'd been talking to Judas, he'd always described this return to Jerusalem as if it were a key part of a campaign. For him, I guess it had looked like the final assault on the establishment.

By now it was clear this wasn't how Jesus saw it. He wasn't going to storm the city with an army; he was going to try and love people to death. My worry was that, if you try to love people like that, you risk ending up dead yourself.

It was hard for a political radical, which was how I had always seen myself, to accept that there might be a different way. But I had come around. The change our nation needed was far deeper than simply making ourselves free from Rome. I could see that now. Systems needed to change but so did hearts.

At the meal, Jesus talked about what was to come; my memory hasn't held on to every detail. However, I remember very clearly how he talked about betrayal and how awful it would be if any of us turned away from the loyalty we had shown him.

It seemed to me he was talking about one of us who was actually at the table. For a moment, I thought about Judas Iscariot but then decided I must be wrong. He'd been such a key part of the organisation. Surely it couldn't be him.

One by one I went through the people in the room in my head (I suspect we were all doing a similar thing). The thought that someone who was eating this meal with our master could also be the one to betray him was simply horrible. But I also realised that, under certain circumstances, it could be any one of us including me. We all had our weaknesses, our off days.

While Jesus said something that I didn't quite catch, Judas got up to leave. Since he had charge of the money, I thought it might be about making some late purchases for the Passover. That was probably why there'd been mention of the need to hurry.

As he walked away, my thought was that it couldn't have been him that Jesus was talking about because he was no longer in the room and clearly had been given work to do for us. I don't think I have ever been more mistaken.

## Where to find this story in your Bible?

- Matthew 26:20–25
- Mark 14:18–21
- John 13:21–29

# Time and place:
## Caiaphas gets his chance

I'd given up on the idea of making an arrest before the main part of the festival began when the knock came on the door.

It was him: the one we'd gambled thirty pieces of silver on. He said he had a time and a place for us. Outside the city and not far from Bethany – an olive grove called Gethsemane. Out of the way, private, secluded: it was what we had asked for.

The problem though was the time. Judas estimated that we needed to be there sometime in the hour before midnight, certainly not much earlier.

'Are you sure of the timing?' I demanded.

He nodded.

It gave us a dilemma. If we were to make an arrest, then we would need to try and arrest our prisoner before the morning broke. Only in that way would we have a chance of finishing the business before the Sabbath began. We certainly didn't want a martyr's body on display for the holiest day of them all.

I stood there calculating my chances. Pilate would need to be briefed immediately if there were to be a Roman execution. He usually trusted my judgement in these matters so that seemed manageable. Then there was the tricky issue of getting the council's agreement to a trial at night. It was almost certain that there would be some Pharisees who wouldn't like the letter of the law stretched in that sort of way. Joseph of Arimathea would be one of them.

It's most improper, he'd be thinking. Only trials for money may be heard after sunset. Trials for someone's life must proceed by day. That would be the complaint. But Joseph was quiet by nature and I was confident I could manage someone like him.

Besides, we are allowed to consider cases of fraud at any time, day or night. Well, this Jesus was a fraud. Whether we convicted him in the dark watches of the night or the middle of the afternoon made no real difference. If he was guilty at one hour, he'd still be guilty at another. Time is irrelevant both to the innocent and the guilty.

Rehearsed in my head like that, I felt I might carry the members of the council with me. It seemed worth the risk, especially if I'd got some form of prior assent from Pontius Pilate, the governor.

So I turned to my servant. 'Ready the temple guard. I will need them shortly.'

'For an arrest?' he asked.

I knew all too well what he was thinking: arrests are made by the witnesses to a crime, not the guard. That's how the system is supposed to work but it was of no use on this occasion.

'Just do what you're told,' I hissed.

'Certainly, sir. As you say.'

Turning around, I took a long hard look at the man who had agreed to sell his master for significantly less than I thought I would have to pay. I didn't like it. Frankly, I didn't like him. There was something there in front of me that I couldn't quite figure out.

If I'd had any choice, I wouldn't have used him. I had a feeling in my bones that he was leading me into a trap. But needs must on some occasions. It was a risk worth taking.

'You'll need to lead my guards to the place.'

He nodded.

'We'll also need a signal so we know we're getting the right one. It's best if it looks natural. How do you people normally greet each other?'

He looked at the floor and then up at me again. 'With the normal Jewish greeting… a kiss.'

'Excellent! Then a kiss it will be.'

## Where to find this story in your Bible?

- John 13:30

# Going wherever:
## Simon Peter makes a claim

I was reclining next to him at the table, relaxed and almost tempted to feel self-important again. Not that I deserved it after the fuss I'd made about the foot washing. I suppose you could say that at least I'd asked about what he was doing while the others had just stared. Except I didn't simply ask; my mouth charged into the situation without giving my brain time to take a breath, let alone think.

So I promised myself I'd do better during the supper itself. I sat quietly for once, taking in all the elements of the evening. There was lamb, bread, bitter herbs, wine. We shared them solemnly and quietly. It was our meal together as his team – the one he had promised. There were also our master's words during the meal, although they were definitely not what we had expected to hear.

'This is my body,' he told us as he tore the bread into pieces, 'broken for you.'

He had done so much, given his time, his love, his strength to us day by day. So, in that way, I thought I knew what he might mean.

'This is my blood,' he added, passing around the sharing cup with the wine in it. 'It is poured out as a solemn promise to you and to many more.'

We looked across at each other. He'd given his whole life in order to make our lives so much more than we ever could have imagined. That was true. But the talk of wine being poured out like blood troubled me.

I was concerned he might be thinking his life was now at serious risk. You could hardly blame him. The whole week had seemed to be a dangerous venture from the start.

My fears were confirmed on our walk to the Mount of Olives after the meal. He told us he'd only be with us for a little longer. Then he stopped unexpectedly and waited until he was sure we were all facing him.

'Love one another as I have loved you,' he told us. 'That's how people will know you follow me.'

It was heartwarming. He made us feel as if we were part of his family, his children rather than just his followers. But he also said that he was going to a place where we couldn't come. That didn't make sense. I'd promised myself that I'd keep quiet at least for this one evening but what he was saying puzzled me so much.

'Lord,' I said, 'where on earth are you going?'

He just repeated what he'd said but added that I would eventually be able to follow him. It made the mystery of it even greater so I ploughed on with my questions.

'Why can't I follow you now? I will lay down my life for you.'

'Will you?' he asked looking long and hard at me.

It was a fair question. I'd said it without really thinking about whether I'd actually be able to do it. Mouth first again. All the same, I felt totally sure this time. I'd said it and I'd carry through on it.

So that's precisely what I told him. Declared that whoever else fell away, I would still be there.

He looked sad, as if I was missing the point in some way, promised me that I had been in his prayers and I would return to him.

I wasn't taking that as an answer. 'I really am ready to go with you to prison and to death. Right now, if necessary.'

He shook his head. 'Tonight, before the cock crows, you will disown me three times.'

'Never,' I told him with the absolute certainty that only comes with stupidity, 'never ever will you find me disowning you.'

I wasn't alone in my confidence. My brother backed me up and the rest joined in as well. We were right behind him whether he chose to believe it or not.

It didn't occur to me that, if I'd got it wrong about a small thing like the feet washing, it was perfectly possible for me to make much, much greater errors as well. I didn't know Jesus as well as I thought I did but, just as bad, I didn't know myself.

## Where to find this story in your Bible?

- Matthew 26:26–35
- Mark 14:22–31
- Luke 22:17–20, 31–34
- John 13:33–38

# Remain in my love:
## Andrew hears and fears

It's difficult when the person you've followed for three years tells your brother he's about to lie repeatedly. Especially when it's about something which had always seemed like the most important thing in the world to him. Peter would disown me before he'd disown Jesus. I'd have bet on it.

But it was the strangest of evenings and perhaps anything was possible. Jesus talked to us about being prepared in a way we had never thought of until that moment: purse, bag, sword. For the first time his instructions were about being able to stand on our own two feet in the bad times ahead. It was as if we might find ourselves alone and need to fight our corner… literally.

He said so much that evening that I wonder if I've remembered even a half of it. But some things stood out.

He knew we were afraid and told us not to be. Easier said than done. He talked about going ahead of us to his Father's house. There are many, many places for you to rest there, he assured us, and I am going to make sure they are ready for each one of you.

It was not entirely clear what he was on about. Both Thomas and Phillip were very puzzled and I'm pretty sure the further explanations didn't make it any clearer.

But I do remember one phrase particularly: 'Do not let your hearts be troubled.' It felt like he was speaking directly to me. When I don't know where things are leading or how I can put right something that I've got terribly wrong, it feels like my chest is being gripped so tight I'll never breathe freely again.

So when he said, 'Do not let your hearts be troubled', I sat very still and took a deep breath which I let out as slowly as I could. It felt a little better.

'When I am gone,' he continued, 'I will still be with you because my spirit will come and live in your hearts. A spirit that makes clear what is true, what is good; a spirit that brings peace. Be comforted: you will still feel like my family, you will still be my family.'

It was reassuring and slightly terrifying all at once. We were to be like branches on a vine. That bit was fine. But we'd also be seeing, then not seeing him, which definitely wasn't fine.

There was more to say, he admitted, but it might be too much. My feeling was he'd already said too much. I had no idea at all how I would cope if he wasn't there to help.

As I tried to control my rising panic, he said four words that I wish I could engrave upon my heart: 'Remain in my love.' If I could only manage that, I could do anything.

At the time, I couldn't imagine how it might happen but Jesus seemed very sure that the spirit he had promised us would make all sorts of things possible. Would it? I hoped before God that it would.

As we walked to the Mount of Olives that evening, I think somewhere deep within me I knew it would be the last time we walked this road together.

## Where to find this story in your Bible?

- Luke 22:35–37
- John 14:1–31; 15:1–10

# Watch:
## Simon Peter wakes up

After we had slipped out of Jerusalem under cover of a starless darkness, we set off down the Kidron Road. Once we were on the far side of the valley, we stopped at an olive grove called Gethsemane. We'd used it regularly. I'd often thought of it as our Lord's peaceful place. Once there, Jesus told us to pray, not for him but for ourselves, for the challenges we were going to meet, the temptations we were going to face.

Then, along with James and John, he took me just a stone's throw further into the garden. We were chosen to be his eyes and ears as he prayed. I always felt honoured when I was included with his two cousins. It was like an inner circle and I felt then that my clumsy words earlier had not broken our friendship.

He told us how he felt overwhelmed, sensed the shadow of death. But the reason he'd taken us with him was so that we could keep watch in case of any danger. Whatever was to happen next, he needed to pray in safety, at least for a little while. No one has ever been given a clearer or more straightforward job than we had that evening. But the week had begun to wear us down; the days had been long and our sleep had been unsettled.

We heard his prayer: 'Abba, Father, let this hour pass from me, let this cup be taken away from me. You can do that. Everything is possible with you.'

It sounded as if he was in agony and I felt so helpless. There was a pause where he seemed to say nothing. Perhaps he was listening or perhaps he was just trying to find the words. Then I heard him eventually say: 'Not what I want, Father, but what you want.' And that was it.

Whatever he may or may not have said after that, I missed because I couldn't keep my eyes open any longer.

The next thing I remember was him shaking my shoulder and saying, 'Simon, could you not keep watch for one hour? Stay awake with me. Pray that you will not drift into temptation. You want to do the right thing but your body is letting you down tonight.'

He'd called me *Simon*, my first name, not *Peter*, the rock. You could hardly blame him for thinking like that. While he was in anguish, I was fast asleep.

How could I have failed so utterly? Because I was exhausted. James and John had dropped off as well but it seemed a whole lot worse for me. I had been chosen to lead; I was also the night fisherman who never lost concentration. If I could do it in a boat, why on earth couldn't I do it for Jesus when he most needed it?

To make it even worse, I kept drifting back to sleep. It was as if I'd reached the end of the road and just wanted to crawl under a safe, warm blanket from where I need never come out. But that wasn't an option. Suddenly I heard my master say, 'the betrayer is here'. In a moment I was wide awake and checking that I was armed.

## Where to find this story in your Bible?

- Matthew 26:36–46
- Mark 14:32–42
- Luke 22:40–46
- John 18:1–2

# The kiss:
## Simon the Zealot watches and wonders

Although I should have been praying in Gethsemane, I found myself wondering whether we were going to get back to Bethany without any mishap. I tried to calculate in my head exactly how long it was going to take us. So, while it may have looked as if I was deep in prayer, it would be truer to say I was worrying. Sometimes those two activities look more similar than they should.

I heard something before I saw anything. When you've been on the edge of what the authorities allow or beyond, you learn to be alert and it never leaves you.

'Here it comes,' I thought, although even I was surprised by the number of temple guards and others who'd been bundled together for this makeshift snatch squad. They were carrying torches, lanterns, swords and clubs. It was as if they'd simply grabbed anything they could.

And, right in the centre of the pack, was Judas. I was horrified and puzzled at the same time, although not as surprised as some because those with a mind for revolution do strange things.

'Rabbi,' he said as he greeted Jesus, 'shalom.' And he kissed him on both cheeks.

As the guards stepped forward, my first thought was what a despicable way to betray a friend. My second was to wonder what on earth he was doing and thinking. Was there some kind of plot within a plot?

The arrest faltered as quickly as it had started because Jesus stepped towards the motley crew sent to arrest him.

'So, who is it you want?' he asked.

'Jesus of Nazareth,' they replied.

'Well, that's me,' he told them. 'I am Jesus of Nazareth.' And they stepped back. Some fell to the ground.

It didn't make sense for a moment, but then I realised. They were terrified. A man who could heal people miraculously and even raise them from the dead might also use such powers in other ways. They were not safe. At least that must have been how it felt.

I looked closely at Judas. Was this what he expected? He seemed to be uncomfortable but he also seemed to be watching intently.

'If you are looking for me, then I am here.' Jesus continued, 'Let the others go.'

That was his red line: our safety rather than his.

But, as the guards stepped forward to arrest him, Simon Peter drew his sword and struck one of the High Priest's servants on the ear. In almost any other circumstance, that would surely have been the signal to unleash bloodshed on a major scale and my hand went to my knife.

Jesus stopped the mayhem before it began. 'No more of this!' he said firmly and healed the servant. Judas Iscariot's mouth dropped open when he saw that as if he didn't know what to think or say or do.

Then Jesus turned to the arresting party, 'Am I leading a rebellion?' he asked. 'Is that why you have come out with swords and clubs to capture me? Every day I was with you, teaching in the temple courtyards and you did absolutely nothing.'

In the blink of an eye he was arrested and the rest of us didn't wait around to see if we were next. As we fled, I was almost certain I saw young John Mark in the shadows on the far side of the olive grove.

Amidst the chaos and the panic, I found myself thinking we were going to be in such trouble with his mother if the boy got arrested. It was only later I found out how close that came to happening.

## Where to find this story in your Bible?

- Matthew 26:47–56
- Mark 14:43–52
- Luke 22:47–53
- John 18:1–11

# Near the fire:
## Simon Peter in the courtyard

When the arrest was made in Gethsemane, we fled. Cowardly, but it did mean that none of us were arrested with him, which is what Jesus had demanded as the price of his surrender. Somehow that made it worse.

Many years later, I asked John Mark whether we did the right thing. Hidden in the shadows, he was the only one who saw the whole scene as it played out. 'It didn't seem you had any choice' was what he told me but it didn't make me feel any better about it.

When we were safely out of sight, some of us slowed down and gathered back together. 'What now?' was the question in all our heads There was a need to warn those in Bethany about what had happened but those in Jerusalem had to be alerted as well. In short, people needed to go in two directions.

The dangerous choice was, of course, Jerusalem. We were marked men in the eyes of the Jewish leaders. If the imprisonment of Jesus turned out not to be enough, then any of us might be next.

I volunteered to go to Jerusalem because I was terrified… and that was the simplest way of facing my fear.

John said he'd go with me as he was known at the high priest's residence. Even Caiaphas had to get his salt fish from somewhere and John had often been the one from his family who travelled between Galilee and the city.

We took the same road as the arrest party back up the Kidron valley and into the city by the old steps near the pool of Siloam. As the high priest's crew climbed through the valley, we could faintly see their outline lit by torches about half a mile ahead. The night kept us hidden in the shadows.

When we reached the high priest's house sometime after the arrest party, John gained entry into the courtyard but I didn't. I could see him saying hello to those he knew and chatting comfortably with them.

My first thought was to be a little jealous at how easy it had been for John to gain entry and how skilfully he managed the social niceties, even though his stomach must have been churning just like mine.

After a few minutes, he came back to the door of the courtyard and spoke to the girl on duty there. She nodded to him and let me in.

It was a cold night for the time of year and a fire had been lit. The servants and the officials who had little to do for the moment gathered round the flames to stay warm. I joined them.

Having got this far, I had no idea at all what to do and John was busy working on his connections. One of the servant girls looked across at me, as if she recognised who I was.

'You were with the prisoner, weren't you? The man from Nazareth?'

'I don't know what you're talking about,' I told her and moved away from the fire towards the gateway. The last thing I wanted was to be the centre of attention.

It didn't work. I heard one of the girls saying, 'This guy was definitely with them.'

They were beginning to look at me closely and, frankly, I panicked.

'Not me,' I declared. 'I swear you've got the wrong man.' It put them off pursuing questions and they left me alone for a little while.

It wasn't the end, though. After a while their curiosity got the better of them. One of those standing nearest to me declared, as if he was absolutely certain, 'You *are* one of them. No doubt about it. Your accent gives you away.'

I was telling them they didn't know what they were going on about, when a cousin of Malchus joined the argument.

Now Malchus was the high priest's servant who I'd attacked in Gethsemane. His cousin was even more certain than the others and I lost it completely – just swore and swore that it wasn't true… even though it was. Then a cock crowed. In my temper, I'd forgotten all about what Jesus had said.

And that was when I saw him – being taken from Caiaphas to Pilate. He looked across, straight at me. I was utterly speechless. Later, people would tell me that I might have imagined it but there he was, as real as he had always been: the very eyes I wanted to avoid but couldn't turn away from.

I left the courtyard as quickly as I could after that. Once outside, I wept and wept and wept.

I hadn't just denied Jesus; I'd turned it into a massive drama in order to convince people who were just curious. They weren't threatening John, who they knew well enough followed Jesus, so why on earth was I so worried they might be threatening me?

I'd spent a whole 24 hours making one mistake after another, saying one wrong thing after another. Useless, weak, stupid!

I'd walked so deep into the darkness I was sure there was no way out. The last thing Jesus would remember about me was my foul-mouthed denial of him.

## Where to find this story in your Bible?

- Matthew 26:57–58, 69–75
- Mark 14:53–54, 66–72
- Luke 22:54–62
- John 18:15–18, 25–27

# The one:
## Caiaphas directs proceedings

'There is a time for every purpose under heaven,' I told my colleagues before we began the trial, 'and tonight we must do our duty for the sake of our nation.'

There was an awkward silence. *They're letting the importance of this sink in,* I told myself. Deep down, I knew the cogs of doubt were turning in the brains of those I had yet to convince. We had at least made a start. I'd left the initial questioning to Annas, my father-in-law. As the previous high priest, he knew the importance of being absolutely clear with any evidence we presented to the Romans.

While he got on with that, I began to gather the ruling council together for the court proceedings and to check we had the witnesses we needed. Neither of those experiences filled me with any great confidence. I felt as if I was dealing almost exclusively with the reluctant and the incompetent.

Annas had not got all that far in my absence. When he'd asked Jesus about what he'd said, the man had the effrontery to raise his eyebrows and tell him he should surely have heard that already as it had all taken place in the temple. To drive his point home, he opened his palms and suggested my father-in-law ask those who had heard him. They were the witnesses. Surely, they would know. One of the officials slapped him for his rudeness and told him it was no way to speak to the previous high priest.

'If I said anything wrong,' he replied, 'testify as to what it is. But, if I didn't, why do you abuse me?'

In short, all my father-in-law had established was that our prisoner knew the law as well as I did. His talk of witnesses and testimony went right to the heart of my difficulty. We'd need a robust combination of both if the conviction was to stand up when presented to Pilate.

Instead, when the trial got under way, there was problem after problem. Witnesses were plentiful, but any coherent story between them was astonishingly absent. Just as I was thinking we were getting nowhere, we heard a witness who claimed Jesus had said he would destroy the temple and rebuild it in three days. It didn't make much sense but it was something. Then we heard another version of this tale. The trouble was that there were several serious differences. What we needed were pieces of evidence that agreed with each other.

Once we had that, we might have a basis on which to convict. All I was currently in possession of was a basis to be laughed at. In desperation, I turned to the prisoner and asked him what he had to say.

I know, I know: Jewish law says that a prisoner must not be asked to convict himself. But it also says he has a right to defend himself. My ploy yielded nothing useful because Jesus remained resolutely silent. But asking him had given me an idea. I decided to use the Oath of Testimony. Any Jewish man or woman is bound by the laws of their faith to answer that.

'Are you the Christ, the one who is to come?' I asked.

He replied, 'It is as you say.'

That's a 'yes' in our language. There was a pause and, in the silence, hope coursed through my veins that I might be nearly there. Then he continued.

'In the future you will see the Son of Man sitting at the right hand of the Mighty One and coming on the clouds of heaven.'

The gasp that went around the room told me that I had what we needed. I tore my clothes to express horror at what had been said and declared, 'Why should we seek any more witnesses? You have heard the blasphemy.'

In that moment, the dubious legality of the process was overwhelmed by the enormity of the claim we had heard. The decision was made – guilty. We didn't have any dissenters at all. That is what I call a result.

As we made arrangements to transfer our prisoner to Pilate, the guards taunted him. They spat in his face, blindfolded him, punched him and demanded he prophesy who had hit him: the sort of thing soldiers do to let off steam.

As we left with our prisoner, I saw him glance across the courtyard. Somehow, one of his disciples seemed to have gained entrance. *That's one brave idiot if ever I saw one*, I thought. But he looked as if he knew the game was up and I was absolutely certain of it.

## Where to find this story in your Bible?

- Matthew 26:59–68; 27:1–2
- Mark 14:53, 55–65; 15:1
- Luke 22:63–71
- John 18:12–14, 19–24

# Late night words:
## Claudia Procula has a dream

They had let me come to what my old friends used to call 'that God-forsaken country' because my grandfather had been the emperor. 'A privilege for a procurator's wife' someone had declared. But, as my mother observed, 'Pilate's only a procurator in the first place because he married you.'

We came to this outpost of the empire because… well, somebody had to. In truth, I had mixed feelings: pleased enough to be able to be with my husband; shocked by how far it was from Rome. It was not quite as bad as I'd imagined. Far from being God-forsaken as my friends had thought, the whole country seemed absorbed by its faith in one god.

I made excellent new friends: good-humoured, thoughtful women who helped me understand how the world worked here. One of those was Joanna, whose husband managed King Herod's household.

She came to mind when Caiaphas visited us late on Thursday night before the Passover. I was surprised that my husband had agreed to meet the high priest at such a late hour. He has a habit of making people wait. However, the Passover Festival is such a charged and potentially dangerous time I guessed he'd decided to hear what the issue was.

The problem was a subversive preacher who some were calling 'the one who would come'. The Jewish guards were about to arrest him and Caiaphas believed that he would probably be found guilty on a capital charge. His concern was that the delicate balance of peace might be blown apart if this man wasn't stopped.

I wouldn't normally be privy to any of this but the meeting was so late it took place in our private rooms. I was thinking as I listened that, whoever this poor fellow was, he had already been thoroughly stitched up.

Then there was mention of the Nazarene and I realised who they were talking about. This was Jesus, the man who had cured Joanna. He wasn't some two-bit revolutionary come to pester a Roman legion; he was a renowned healer and teacher.

Of course that didn't seem to come into the equation with either Caiaphas or Pilate. They were too busy talking about keeping the peace, which of course meant making their lives quiet and comfortable.

Naturally, I didn't say anything. I knew better than most how stubborn my husband could be if challenged. But it troubled me to think how little one man's life seemed to count for in this country.

I didn't hear exactly what they had agreed but they were quickly nodding to each other and then Caiaphas was scurrying away as if his purity would be soiled if he stayed a moment longer than he had to.

I didn't sleep well that night. Sadly, it's often like that when we're in Jerusalem. The air closes in on you somehow. And, on this occasion, I dreamt in a way I don't remember ever happening before.

I'd seen the Nazarene preacher once or twice because of my friendship with Joanna and suddenly he was there in my dreams. I kept reaching out to him and every time my fingertips were nearly there a wind seemed to take him out of reach.

It was one of those dreams where you never reach the place you want to be whatever you do. And it was so real. I woke in a cold sweat and knew that I would not sleep again that night.

My husband was up even before me. I wondered if he'd dreamt something too but I doubted it. So I decided to send a note to him: *Don't get mixed up in condemning that innocent man. I've spent a long night troubled by a dream about him.*

To be honest, I didn't think it would do any good. Politics has always placed general necessity above individual people. But I hoped and prayed that he'd find a way to calm the unrest without hanging an innocent man on a cross. For once it wasn't the country that felt forsaken, it was me.

## Where to find this story in your Bible?

- Matthew 27:19
- Luke 8:1–3

# FRIDAY

# Crossing the line:
## Joseph of Arimathea thinks again

There are moments in life when you realise that someone you've held to be a close colleague has crossed a line and things will never ever be the same.

The previous night, I had watched Caiaphas manoeuvre Jesus into condemning himself. My mouth dropped open when I realised what he was doing. But I had said nothing. Then Jesus talked about coming on the clouds of heaven and I knew he was lost. After that, there wasn't even a formal vote. The council had agreed unanimously about his guilt.

Actually, that's not quite right. Neither Nicodemus nor I thought the case had been properly heard but a tide of prejudice against this strange and wonderful man had somehow swept us along. Now I was standing outside Pilate's residence as the council presented their prisoner to the governor.

I was not essential to this part of the process but I was determined to be there in case there was any chance to redeem myself and ensure, even at this late stage, a proper legal process. It seemed unlikely. According to Caiaphas, the governor had already agreed to rubber stamp our decision in order to ensure a peaceful Passover. Although, how a killing creates peace has never been explained to me.

We stood outside the palace while Jesus was taken to Pilate. This allowed us to maintain our strict rules about observing the Passover Festival. Although such strict adherence to rules hadn't seemed to bother any of us a short while earlier.

Pilate came out on to the balcony that overlooked the street.

'What charges are you bringing against this man?' he asked.

That completely wrong-footed Caiaphas and his team. Pilate had been told earlier what the accusation was and the council had merely expected to confirm publicly to the governor that they'd found the prisoner guilty.

Instead, Pilate had begun as if he was going to do things properly, in the correct Roman fashion. For a moment, hope rose again for this man I had admired so secretly.

The reply from the street to Pilate was a mixture of astonishment and barely concealed rudeness. 'We wouldn't have handed him over to you if he weren't a criminal.'

You don't talk to the Roman procurator like that. A thin smile curled around his lip for just a moment. Then it disappeared. 'Seeing as you find him to be a criminal, take him away and use your laws to make a judgement.'

'Brilliant,' I thought. He wants us to deal with it and we've no authority to impose a death penalty. He'll be imprisoned and we'll be able to find a way to reopen the case.

Some of the teachers of the law pointed this out to Pilate.

Then Caiaphas' men began, under his whispered instructions, to make up accusations that would rattle the governor. 'Perverting our nation', which was the first accusation, seemed weak. The Roman Empire is always perfectly happy to see us squabble among ourselves.

The second accusation was more serious. They shouted that he had forbidden us to pay taxes to Caesar. Almost the opposite was true but Pilate didn't know that.

In all of this, Jesus said nothing. Pilate looked back towards him several times but I never heard him utter a single syllable. Perhaps he thought silence was his best defence or perhaps he felt it would be a waste of words.

Finally, they yelled that he had been claiming to be king. That was the most serious charge. It's the Romans who decide who may or may not be king. It's their system we live under, not ours. If we started taking things into our own hands, you'd soon smell the whiff of revolution and right after that you'd be able to hear the march of Roman soldiers come to crush it.

Pilate stood still for a moment, looked down at us as if he didn't trust a single person in the whole crowd. Then he turned on his heel and marched like the soldier he was back into the palace.

Obviously he had retreated in order to speak to the prisoner himself. If we hadn't insisted on being so exact about religious observance, Caiaphas might have been able to be there in person to make his part of the case. Instead, we were all left outside.

I looked across at our high priest and thought that at last he was experiencing what it's like to be an outsider, just like the man he was so keen to persecute.

## Where to find this story in your Bible?

- John 18:28–31
- Matthew 27:12
- Luke 23:1–2

# Inside the palace:
## Pilate meets the prisoner

I stared at the prisoner: anyone less like a soldier, let alone a terrorist, was hard to imagine. He was a bit weather-beaten and obviously exhausted but there was quietness about him that you might expect to find in a scholar. I'd have placed him in a library not on trial for his life.

'So what did you do before all this started?' I asked.

'Carpentry,' he told me. 'Anything with wood and anything with buildings – if it needed mending, I would do it.'

I was trying, for once, to fix in my mind what I was dealing with here. My wife's note about her dream had made me curious; otherwise, I'd have simply waved the execution through without a thought. I'm not a romantic.

'You've heard what your own people have accused you of and you've said precisely nothing. Frankly, that amazes me. *Are* you the king of the Jews?'

He answered my question with a question. Nobody does that to a Roman governor!

'Is that your own idea?' he asked. 'Or did others talk to you about me?'

Somehow he's found out about my conversation with Caiaphas, I thought. Of course he could have been talking about the rabble who had yelled about him from the street but I doubted that.

'Am I a Jew?' I replied. The idea amused me faintly. I've been many things over the years but Jewish isn't one of them.

'Look,' I told him. 'It was your people, your chief priests who handed you over to me. I still don't get what is going on here. What is it that you have actually done?'

His answer astonished me. He wasn't denying he was a king but he told me that it had nothing to do with the streets and alleyways of Jerusalem or anywhere else on this earth. A sort of heavenly kingdom, I thought to myself. Naturally I don't believe in such things.

He clearly reckoned he had enough power behind him to make a fight of it but told me the kingdom he was actually willing to fight for was something else entirely. Frankly, his answer had not taken me much further forward. On the other hand, it seemed fairly clear he was not dangerous, only strange.

'You are a king, then?' I suggested.

He agreed but went on to talk about being a king of truth whose followers were with him because they too were on the side of truth. It sounded a bit weird but that's all.

'What is truth?' I asked him but I wasn't really seeking an answer. I just didn't want him thinking I'd actually swallowed his view of the world.

However, I'd made up my mind: he was harmless enough. I nodded to the guards and returned to the balcony. The rabble outside were furious when I told them that I had failed to establish a charge against him. They yelled and jeered; said he'd been causing trouble all over Judea.

One of them shouted, 'He started the trouble in Galilee. Now he's brought it all the way here.'

That gave me an idea. Galilee was Herod's province. Herod was in Jerusalem. Surely, he'd be only too delighted to exercise his powers. So that's where I sent him.

My wife, of course, was delighted that I hadn't condemned this rabbi to death but less impressed by the fact that I'd sent him to Herod.

'Claudia,' I said. 'You understand better than most what this land is like. I'm not a miracle worker.'

'No,' she said rather sadly. 'He is.'

## Where to find this story in your Bible?

- John 18:33–38
- Luke 23:3–7

# Amuse me:
## Joanna watches a circus

When your husband is the one responsible for the whole of Herod's royal household and all that goes on within it, you get used to very strange happenings and, sometimes, you see the most grotesque things imaginable. It's not a good place to be.

'This is my job,' Chuza would explain to me, when he felt uncomfortable about what he had to do. 'It's what puts food on our table and on the tables of everyone else who works here. I do my best to contain and calm down situations that the king may regret when he wakes up the next morning but I can only do so much.'

I understood him well enough but it was also why I was happiest when I could be away from the palace. I loved the open air, my good friends and, best of all, listening quietly to the teacher who had healed me.

The thought had never entered my mind that the worlds I knew inside and outside of the palace might one day collide. It happened on a Friday in Passover Week.

'They're bringing a prisoner called Jesus of Nazareth across from Pilate's residence,' one of the young servant girls told me.

I was shocked. I didn't even know he'd been arrested. On the other hand, I wasn't surprised. The gossip had been saying it was only a matter of time before something happened. I'd been silently praying each night that the rumours would turn out to be false.

When they brought him into Herod's presence, I was horrified. Jesus looked so drawn, so pale, as if he hadn't slept for a month, never mind just a night. It was as if the weight of the world was on his shoulders and he was slowly being crushed under the pressure.

This was the man who had healed me. Without him, I wouldn't have been at Herod's court that morning… or indeed anywhere else. My sheer existence was testimony to his healing power.

Of course, all Herod wanted from him was amusement. He'd heard about the miracles and had long fancied seeing some of them for himself. On one occasion, he had called me into his room to hear more about what 'the man from Nazareth' could do. I told him my story as honestly as I could but he lost interest halfway through. It wasn't exciting enough for him.

For me, of course, it was the difference between life and death or, at least, that was how it felt. And it was certainly the reason I became a follower and a helper to him.

The Jesus I grew to know was strong, loving, witty and generous with his time to those he met. Nobody felt excluded; nobody felt short-changed.

So, to see him brought in and pushed around as a prisoner-cum-clown was almost unbearable. Herod, of course, demanded miracles. He was particularly keen to see him turn water into wine. No surprise in that. Jesus said nothing, standing like a silent ghost lost in a theatre of madness.

At the same time, there was also an avalanche of allegations about him from the chief priests and the teachers of the law who had arrived shortly after the prisoner. I doubt if Herod heard any of them. He was too interested in getting his prize exhibit from Pilate to do something that would entertain him.

When it was clear that there would be no such thing, they were reduced to making fun of him. And when that became boring too, they dressed him in the most elegant robe they could find.

I wondered just for a moment whether Herod was about to find him innocent or guilty. In either case it would have been without taking any notice of the evidence. Instead, he sent him back to Pilate with a note to say how kind he'd been to let him meet this so-called wonder-worker.

That, of course, left Pilate with the judgement still to make. I wasn't surprised. Herod would never make a hard decision if it could be palmed off on someone else.

Jesus was taken away with much pushing, shoving and jeering. All I could do was watch the abuse. It was a scene that has never left my mind: the kindest human I had ever met treated like a figure of fun on a holiday weekend. For the man who had healed me, it looked very much like the end of all hope.

## Where to find this story in your Bible?

- Luke 8:1–3; 23:8–12

# The price:
## Pilate's hand is forced

It came as no surprise that Herod sent Jesus back to me when he'd lost interest in him. The old fox would never take responsibility for something if he could avoid it. Still, he was pleased to have met him and it healed the rift between us which proved to be a significant advantage in the years to come. But it was no good to me on that Friday morning. So I called Caiaphas and his motley crew back to meet me again. I'd had enough.

'I have examined this man in your presence,' I told the crowd that had been gathering. 'And I have found no basis for your charges against him. Herod has also been given an opportunity to review the matter and has come to the same conclusion as I have. It is clear that he has done nothing that deserves the death penalty. Therefore I will punish and then release him. This is the Passover; that is our custom.'

On any other day in my time as procurator, that would have been the end of it and for a second or two I thought it was. Then I heard a voice say, 'Barabbas; we want Barabbas.' As long as it was a lone voice, I could ignore it. But others joined in, 'Barabbas; we want Barabbas.' The volume grew.

Of course I knew they had little interest in the troublemaker and murderer who they were shouting for. They'd probably been put up to it by the priests who envied the influence that the man from Galilee was having.

'What shall I do with the one you call the king of the Jews?' I asked. By this stage, I was willing to release two prisoners rather than one if it calmed the situation.

'Crucify him!' they yelled back at me. 'He claims to be the Son of God; he must die.'

I withdrew from the balcony to the palace in the hope that my absence might help to damp down the storm that seemed to be building. And I looked again at the man who had somehow let loose this mad fire of hatred among the people in the city.

'Where do you come from?' I asked. He didn't answer me. 'Don't you realise I have the power to release you… or crucify you?'

'You would have no power over me,' he said, 'unless it were given to you from above. The greater sin lies with the one who handed me over to you.'

He spoke so calmly, so certainly that it unsettled me. There are very many in this land for whom I have no interest in whether they live or die. But he wasn't one of them. It seemed to me that Claudia might be right about the man in front of me and I determined to free him if I could.

It wasn't to be. The crowd had been whipped into a frenzy and my return to the balcony made it worse. The cry of 'crucify him' was picked up again and shouted rhythmically like a crowd at a Roman amphitheatre. They were baying for blood and suggesting that my loyalty to Rome was in question.

I raised my hand and they quietened for a moment. 'What crime has he committed?' I demanded to know.

It was useless. I might as well have been telling the sea to turn back or the desert wind to change direction. The note that my wife had sent me was in the back of my mind and I could see no reason why I should take the responsibility for this man's death. Herod hadn't. Why on earth should I?

I called for a bowl of water and a towel. The uproar paused a little as if they were curious about what I was doing. So, very slowly and ceremonially, I washed my hands. The Jews understood a gesture like that and there was a growing sense of expectation in the momentary quiet.

As I took the towel from my servant, I declared that this man's blood was on their hands not mine.

They yelled back their delight that his death should be their responsibility and their children's responsibility. It struck me as a very odd way to practise any religion, but I released Barabbas to them and handed Jesus over to my soldiers.

Claudia was appalled at what had happened and I was furious to have been manoeuvred into a position where keeping the peace for Caesar meant letting some tiny nation's savage politicians have their way.

'Could nothing else be done?' Claudia asked me.

'It is the price of Empire,' I told her.

## Where to find this story in your Bible?

- Matthew 27:15–25
- Mark 15:6–15
- Luke 23:13–25
- John 18:39–40; 19:1–16

# Handed over:
## Joseph of Arimathea hears the verdict

The word came back to the temple that Herod had finished examining Jesus and he was back with Pilate. We were required again. It was difficult to decide whether that was good news or bad. The recall, at least in my mind, held out the possibility that a final judgement had not yet been made.

I joined those gathered around Caiaphas to return to the street outside the palace. As far as the council was concerned, I was still a loyal member of that inner circle. In my heart, I realised I'd become anything but.

If Caiaphas was expecting a quick agreement to his wishes from the governor, he was thoroughly disappointed. 'Not guilty' was Pilate's verdict, apparently backed up by Herod on this occasion. Even worse for the chief priest, Pilate was planning to release the prisoner.

*Passover*, I thought. Well, of course, he nearly always releases someone at Passover. What a neat way to sidestep the council!

The trouble was that it gave Caiaphas an idea. 'Shout for Barabbas' he told some in the crowd he'd gathered for his purposes.

They did. And when Pilate asked them about Jesus, they didn't even need prompting but screamed 'Crucify him!' like a pack of dogs that had sensed a kill.

The colour drained from Pilate's face. Mind you, he wasn't one to give up easily or change his position without a fight. The argument swung back and forth but without the crowd taking much notice of what he had to say.

This is what Caiaphas wants, I thought to myself. The more this goes on and the angrier the crowd becomes the closer we'll get to a riot.

The most astonishing thing of all was hearing a crowd gathered by the high priest yelling, 'We have no king but Caesar!' It was as if the whole world had been turned upside down.

What surprised me in all this was how Pilate sought every possible route to extract himself from what I was sure he would usually have just nodded through.

I didn't know at that moment what Joanna told me later about Claudia Procula's dream. While Pilate would happily hate almost anyone who crossed his path, he loved her and knew how much his position depended on her connections.

Eventually, Pilate could see no way out of the dilemma he'd got himself into. I think it was the cry from the crowd that if he released Jesus, he was no friend of Caesar's which made him act.

Before he did, though, he washed his hands of the affair. Or at least he did in public. My guess is that the gesture was for his wife's benefit: to keep peace in his own household as well as in the city.

In reality, there could be no absolving yourself as governor. The execution was on his watch and at his authorisation.

Jesus was flogged and then dragged away to his fate.

I had been in the wrong place at the wrong time before but nothing until that day had come close to the horror of those moments.

As they led him to Skull Hill, I assumed my pitiful part in all this was over. And that shows you how hard it is to guess what will come next in your life.

## Where to find this story in your Bible?

- Matthew 27:15–26
- Mark 15:6–15
- Luke 23:13–24
- John 18:39–40; 19:7–16

# Those who don't belong:
## Caiaphas in a charitable mood

I had never got to know a great deal about what Jesus had to say but I do remember being told that he had once said how you needed to love your enemies. I felt flattered that he spoke so positively about me. And, for once, I could agree with him but perhaps not quite in the sense he meant it.

You see, I had no choice about who I treated as a friend. Everyone who I worked with had to be kept onside. In private, I could loathe them. In public, I had to love them, massage their egos, keep them sweet… especially in the case of the Romans.

I thought I'd made a good job of getting alongside Pontius Pilate. 'The common interest' was the phrase I used. Although, when I got back to the temple after we'd finally got the Nazarene condemned, I was seething with anger about the way Pilate had seemed to twist and turn that morning. Still, we'd got there in the end.

Then *he* turns up – not Pilate but the disciple with the darting eyes we'd used to arrest Jesus in the first place. *What on earth can he want?*, I asked myself. *Probably more money on the basis he's delivered the goods.*

It turned out to be exactly the opposite. He seemed shocked that the legal process had run its course so swiftly and his ex-boss was going to be crucified. The fool was desperate to turn back the clock. Life isn't like that. He told us he had sinned. Well, that's something we all have to deal with from time to time.

'I've betrayed an innocent man,' he declared, looking around wildly as if he might find a solution in some corner of the room.

I almost pointed out to him that he'd come to us in the first place and not the other way round. Instead we told him that it was his problem and no concern of ours.

That was when he threw the money at us: all thirty pieces of silver. It was an even more impressive performance than Pilate washing his hands but it didn't make any difference. I looked at this strange creature we'd done a deal with and shrugged my shoulders. There was nothing I could do and, pretty obviously, nothing he could do.

I'm told that, after he left us, he went and hanged himself. It made the fact he'd given up his master to us so willingly even more puzzling. I have a suspicion he had been attempting to precipitate chaos and revolution by his betrayal. If he was, he'd made exactly the wrong calls. You have to calculate carefully if you want to get your hands into the politics of this country.

It left us with the dilemma of what to do with the money he'd thrown at us. We couldn't simply put it back into the temple treasury. It was tainted and I was always a stickler for the rules. So we had to get rid of it in another way. One colleague suggested we use it buy a cemetery for foreigners who died in our city. We'd talked about it before but had been reluctant to use temple money for such purposes.

However, the blood money which Judas didn't want – that was a different matter. The idea cheered me up no end. You know, it's always a good idea to have somewhere to bury those who don't belong.

## Where to find this story in your Bible?

- Matthew 27:3–10

# The execution party:
## Albus, soldier on duty

When we arrived in Jerusalem, Quintillus, my commanding officer, gave me one piece of advice. 'You won't like everything you have to do here but you just have to get on with it. That's a soldier's lot. Bite your tongue and think of home.'

Life in the city started with weeks of routine guard duty and very little else. The dance party around the rabbi on a donkey was about as newsworthy as it got. Then there were two sets of crucifixions in a week.

I got through the first by concentrating on my role in the team effort as I usually did. The next one was harder. I listened as I was told what we would be doing that Friday morning and my heart sank – it included the rabbi with the dancing followers. I thought to myself: how quickly things change.

The process was the same as it always was. We were sent for, stripped the prisoner, tied his hands high above his head on the flogging post and proceeded to shred the skin on his back, legs and buttocks.

The flagellum has a large bunch of leather thongs but what makes it cruel are the small pieces of iron and sheep's bone which not only bruise but also shred the flesh.

If you don't know who you're doing this to, it's not so bad but when you realise it's the preacher whose main crime seemed to have been annoying the religious authorities, it's tough. By the time we'd finished, he was in a bad shape, his skin in ribbons and blood everywhere. The message had been to do a particularly thorough job on this one.

After that, he was dressed up as a king: a staff in his hand for the sceptre and a crown of thorns on his head. It dug into his skull and blood streamed down his face and his back. He took it all, said nothing. Then one of the execution team grabbed the staff and beat him mercilessly about the head with it.

It was clear to me that this prisoner wouldn't be able to carry the crucifixion cross-piece all the way to Skull Hill and I was right. He didn't get more than a hundred yards or so.

That's when we grabbed a so-called volunteer – my job, on this occasion.

'Caesar requires your service,' I told a passer-by. 'What's your name?'

He said he was Simon and came from Cyrene. I got the impression he knew about the man we were crucifying. Anyway, he didn't make as much fuss about carrying the cross as some of those we commandeered. As it is with executions, there was a crowd and several women weeping. The prisoner told them not to weep for him but for the troubles to come. It was the first thing I'd heard him say.

There were two others being crucified at the same time. I think the bosses must have been clearing out the troublemakers before the Passover began. When we got to Skull Hill, we tied our prisoner to his place and, on this occasion, nailed his hands to the cross-piece. I never quite found out why we sometimes did that. It was I suspect an extra layer of pain when the situation, for some reason, required it.

The notice attached to the cross for this prisoner said: JESUS OF NAZARETH, THE KING OF THE JEWS. The temple authorities made a big fuss to the governor about that but I'm told that Pilate just scowled at them and declared, 'What I've written stays written.'

The part that really stuck in my mind though was what happened next. As we hung this man on the cross and hauled the post upright, he prayed, 'Father, forgive them for they do not know what they are doing.'

What kind of terrorist or threat to national security prays like that? We were killing a man who didn't deserve a fraction of the things we were doing to him. All I could hope in return for his prayer was that he wouldn't last too long.

We divided out his clothes as we always did on these occasions – one piece each – but my heart wasn't in it. That left the cloak: it was too nice to cut into pieces. We drew lots for it and I won. Exactly what I hoped wouldn't happen. So I took it but at the first opportunity I gave it to a beggar who needed warmth against the night. It was the only moment in the whole day when I felt I'd done something right.

## Where to find this story in your Bible?

- Matthew 27:26–38
- Mark 15:15–26
- Luke 23:26–34
- John 19:16–24

# The not knowing:
## Andrew waits in Bethany

After breakfast in Bethany that Friday morning, I sat with my head in my hands. Martha thought I was praying.

'I'm beyond that,' I told her, feeling a little shamed.

'It might turn out all right.'

'And the sun might set in the east this evening. But I don't think it will and I don't expect any good news today. How's Mary?'

'My sister's praying at the moment, asking again and again why this has been allowed to happen. Mostly, she's been crying quietly.'

Some of the disciples had slept out on the Mount of Olives that night and some of us had retreated to Bethany. I guess we thought we might be safer spread out during the hours of darkness. That way at least some of us might survive.

The morning saw us back together again but with no news from the city and no plan of what to do. We assumed that Jesus would be in prison but there was the unspoken fear that it might be worse than that.

For me, I wanted to know that my brother was safe. James, of course, felt the same.

'At least John has good contacts in Jerusalem,' I told him, 'and he'll know how to use them.'

'Possibly,' James admitted, 'but it's the not knowing that's eating away at me.'

'One or two of us could slip back to the city.'

Neither James nor any of the other disciples said anything in reply to that. We'd agreed to leave the work in Jerusalem to Peter and John because it made no sense for all of us to put our lives at risk. The silence made me imagine my brother chained to a dungeon wall, waiting for the jailer's footsteps that would mean he'd be dragged away to his fate. Not having any news does that sort of thing.

'Use me,' someone said.

I looked up. It was Bartimaeus.

'Nobody knows me. And, if I look like a beggar, nobody will want to know me either. I don't only know about not seeing; I'm also pretty well-versed in not being seen. For once in my life, I'm the best qualified one here.'

I could see his point.

'But what can you do?' James asked.

'Probably not a lot, but I can find out what's been going on. I know where John Mark and Mary live so I can start there. However good or bad the news may be, I can be the messenger.'

So he trudged off up the road. As I watched him disappear into the distance, I offered up a short prayer of thanks for the invisible people who can work without being noticed.

A week ago, when we'd been enjoying the cheering crowds and the palm branches, I'd relished the fact that we were the centre of attention. Now, I longed to be ordinary again and live without anyone asking who I was or who I knew.

## Where to find this story in your Bible?

- Matthew 26:56b
- Mark 14:50

# No way around it:
## Bartimaeus on the road

When you're walking with others, time passes; if you're on your own, it can drag. And it certainly did on that morning. Although I was grateful to be of use to my new friends, the story I'd be carrying back to Bethany surely wouldn't be good.

As I entered Jerusalem, it felt much emptier than it had on the day I'd walked there with Mary. The business of a place begins to drop off on the day before a solemn festival but this seemed more than that, as if people had withdrawn to their homes to stay out of the way. Of course, it probably wasn't like that, just my own unease at work.

I found Mary's house without a problem and John Mark was quietly reading in a shaded corner. He seemed quieter than the last time I'd been there but when he heard my footsteps, he looked up and smiled wearily.

'Have you come in from Bethany?' he asked.

'I have indeed. Are you well?'

'Just about.'

Mary appeared. 'And only *just about*. Did you hear about his escapade?'

'I heard he was at Gethsemane when I suspect he was supposed to be in bed.'

'Tell Bartimaeus what happened.'

Looking embarrassed and awkward, he confessed to his adventure.

'I didn't mean any harm. I was wide awake and heard them leaving. Judas had already gone and I wondered what was going on so I thought I'd follow them.'

'In your nightwear,' his mother added.

'Well, I was in a hurry and I didn't want to miss anything. The city gates are hardly ever locked at this time of year so I thought I'd be able to slip in and out without anybody noticing.'

'And what did you see?' I asked him.

'Prayer, mostly. It was a bit boring. Everyone seemed to be worried about something. Then I heard what sounded like the footsteps of guards – they walk differently to others you know.'

'And you were right.'

'It was too late for me to warn anyone. So I just hid myself out of the way and, after they'd arrested Jesus, I tried to follow them.'

'Brave of you… but possibly quite stupid.'

'One of the guards spotted a movement in the shadows and got a grip on me. I wriggled free and ran for my life. They had too much on their hands to follow.'

'And tell Bartimaeus *exactly* how you wriggled free.' His mother had both hands on her hips as she delivered this demand.

'Er, well they grabbed me by the night cloth I was wearing but it was loose so I let it unravel and sprinted away.'

The penny dropped. 'So you ran home stark naked!'

'But I was safe.'

'Safe, possibly,' his mother said, 'but I have never been so ashamed and embarrassed in my whole life.'

'And also relieved,' I suggested.

'I've lost his father; I can't afford to lose him. Tell him how important he is to me. He doesn't get it when I say it.'

I put my arm around John Mark's shoulders, 'Your mum's right. You're very special and you need to take good care of yourself for everyone's sake. It's not a nice world you're growing up in. If you'd ever begged, you'd know how few really good men and women are out there. But you will find some. We found Jesus, didn't we? All of us. And it matters more than you probably understand as of yet. That's how it is with Jesus.'

'Do you know?' asked Mary.

'Know what?'

'About Jesus… the crucifixion.'

She had to say that last word twice – my mouth dropped open and no words came out. There was no conceivable way it could have happened with that kind of speed.

It wasn't possible. And yet Mary told me that he hung on a cross at Skull Hill even as we sat there talking.

'That's why I followed,' John Mark explained. 'I told Peter that, too. I said I'd have saved him if I could.'

I nodded, 'Of course you would.'

'Peter just burst into tears when I said I'd have saved him if I could. I thought I'd said something wrong but he told me I'd done better than he had.' Mark paused for a moment. 'It wasn't enough though. Nothing anyone could do was enough.'

He was right. I still couldn't quite believe what I'd heard. We were losing the one who made the difference in our lives and were powerless to stop it.

Even though it looked as if there was nothing to be usefully done, I couldn't return to Bethany without being able to tell them I had at least been with Jesus in his suffering, however terrible that might be.

After breaking bread together, I bid Mary and John Mark farewell and braced myself for Skull Hill.

You must understand that, up until then, I'd heard of crucifixions and the cruelty they involved but my blindness meant I'd never seen such an event.

So to watch three men on crosses struggling for their every breath as their bodies were stretched to breaking point was a horror beyond my worst imaginings.

Several of the women who followed were there, including his mother. I wondered how she could bear it. They welcomed me but said hardly anything. I understood. What was there to say? John gave me a great big hug; asked about his brother and the others. At least I could reassure him that they were all safe.

Jesus had been hung in the middle. I suppose it was because, in the eyes of his enemies, he was the prize exhibit. The other two were offenders of a different sort – revolutionaries, terrorists, robbers. Call them what you will – and that may depend on your point of view – they weren't the threat Jesus was. He wanted to see the whole system changed and, for a moment at least, it had seemed as if it might happen.

When I was by the cross, the other two being crucified spoke to Jesus briefly. One abused him like most of the onlookers did.

'Some Messiah you've turned to be!' he complained. 'For crying out loud, save yourself and save us into the bargain.'

The other criminal told him to stop. 'Have you no shame? No fear of God? We've got what we deserved. He hasn't. He's done nothing.' Then he added, 'Jesus, remember me when you're entering that kingdom.'

I waited for an answer. I didn't even know if there would be one. It came interrupted by a ragged breath.

Jesus simply told him that today he would be with him in paradise.

It became dark soon after that, even though it should surely have been around noon. The shadows spooked me. I didn't think I could bear to be at the place of execution much longer and my role as messenger gave me an excuse to get back.

Before I left, I asked John if he had anything to say to his brother.

'Just let him know I'm fine. Mum is, too.'

I looked at him and Salome and thought the one word I wouldn't use to describe them was *fine*. When I got back, I actually told James they were safe which seemed a little more believable and, for the moment at least, not untrue.

The return journey to Bethany meant that I had plenty of time to think. On that afternoon of dark shadows, I wondered if I could make my report of what was happening less painful. John Mark had made it home; Peter and John were still free men; Salome and the three Marys were by the cross, proving yet again how brave they could be.

But the crucifixion: what could I say? I'd tell them that Jesus remained the amazing man he had always been and his eyes were firmly fixed on paradise.

It didn't sound quite so awful if I described it like that. But what I was actually remembering was the terrible suffering I'd seen. They'd look at me when I got back and my eyes would give away any attempts of comfort I tried to bring them. On that Friday, the truth felt horrible and there was no way at all to get round it.

### Where to find this story in your Bible?

- Mark 14:51–52; 15:27–30
- Luke 23:39–44

# Dark skies:
## John takes Mary home

When I saw Bartimaeus briefly on Skull Hill, I couldn't think what to say at first so I just held him tight, pleased and relieved to see someone. Then, I asked him about how they were in Bethany. Were they safe?

As I did, I thought about what this must all be like for him. A new disciple, just able to see again and faced with the worst possible news to take back to the others. I didn't envy that job in the slightest.

I explained how I needed to stay in the city and he understood. But I felt like I was apologising for not joining him. It's stupid to think like that. No one person can be everywhere. But some days you feel you ought to be.

We had actually owned a small house in Jerusalem for as long as I could remember. 'The business requires it', my father, Zebedee, used to say. And my mum, Salome, liked the city almost as much as the lake. I was more ambiguous.

The house was useful when I was sent to trade our salt fish, and I'd made good friends over the years. For all that, I breathed easier when I got out of the city.

On that Friday morning, even before the execution, it had felt especially dark and claustrophobic. We knew all too well what was coming.

Peter had sat in the corner looking beaten and lost. As for my mother, she kept saying, 'Are you sure?' – as if she couldn't quite believe the sentence Pilate had passed on Jesus. Her sister, Mary, said nothing. Not surprising. It was her son we were talking about. There is no worse possible news than the death of the child you gave birth to.

Mary Magdalene was with us as well. She and Salome had worked hard together that week. The details they had toiled to get right for Jesus now seemed small and insignificant. Suddenly I wished that none of us had bothered with anything.

It was Mary Magdalene who broke the inaction. 'There are things we should do,' she declared. 'Things we must do.'

'Like what?' said Peter.

'Some of us need to be there with him.'

Peter winced. I understood why.

'More than that,' she continued, 'I need to be with him. He must know I will always be beside him.'

'It may not necessarily be good for you to do that,' Peter told her.

'Are you saying you think I can't manage?' she snapped back, glaring at him.

'No, no. It's just I think it may be too much for you.'

'You mean I'm weak and liable to fall apart.'

'I didn't say that.'

'But you thought it. He didn't start calling me Magdalene just because I'm tall; he knew how strong he'd made me as well. It was his way of telling me to stay strong. I have to show him I still am. I've got no choice.' She paused but none of us interrupted her. 'Yes, I'm afraid of what might happen but not so afraid that I won't be there beside him.'

Peter said nothing. He knew his own weaknesses well enough and we all recognised he was potentially the next target for the authorities. Peter was safer out of the way on a day like today. He needed time to recover, too. It was hard to imagine how anyone could ever have had a worse 24 hours.

A knock on the door meant that Mary, the wife of Cleopas, had arrived as she had promised she would. The women huddled together for a minute or two and then made to leave.

'If we can do nothing else,' Mary Magdalene said as she went out through the door, 'we will be there with him and we can grieve for all that we have lost.' With that, she left at the head of the party.

The departure seemed to have happened with remarkable haste. Perhaps it was because they feared we might try to stop them. We wouldn't have. The strength was with them that morning.

I turned to Peter, 'Will you try to join them?'

He shook his head.

'Sensible,' I assured him. 'Your name will be at the top of their list if they have such a thing. We don't want to lose you, too.'

He stared at the floor. 'I can't face him. I don't how I would ever have been able to face him again. And now that can never happen. I saw him look at me in the courtyard and I will carry that moment to my grave.'

I couldn't say anything. There were no consoling words to offer, no way to undo what had been done. I just sat there with him. It sounds like the sort of thing a good friend might do but that wasn't the whole reason.

In truth, I was scared as well. What if their list extended to me? Would I be crucified, too? I was not quite as much in the public eye as Peter but I was certainly known.

While I'd not made quite the same noise about following Jesus to the ends of the earth, I'd quietly assumed I might show some courage if I needed to. That was the theory. Now I knew how different and terrifying life can be when it actually happens.

Oddly, it was thinking about my mum that gave me strength. If she could be there with her sister, couldn't I be there, too? It was probably a greater risk for me but I held on to the thought that, if I disappeared, some of my friends in the city would ask questions. And a few of them, at least, were well-known and influential.

Telling Peter I'd be back in a while, I headed out to Skull Hill. I heard the noise of the crowd before I saw the scene. People were jeering and making fun out of the allegation that Jesus had said he'd pull down and rebuild the temple in only three days. Then they were yelling at him to come down from the cross if he was such a miracle worker.

'You saved others,' shouted one fearsome bystander, 'but you can't save yourself.'

That was the behaviour the Roman occupiers encouraged at their executions. Sadly, I wasn't shocked. It all happened only too regularly in Jerusalem. The worse it felt, the better the deterrent: that was Caesar's plan.

'He trusts in God,' yelled another. 'Well, let God rescue him now if he actually wants him.'

There was so much abuse I closed my ears to much of it. Instead I tried to comfort my mother and my aunt. To be honest, I think they comforted me more than I did them.

I don't think Jesus saw us standing together in a group at first. You'd have forgiven him if he hadn't spotted us at all, given the mind-numbing pain he must have been in.

But he did see us and, gathering a little breath as best he could, he said to Mary, 'Here is your son, now.' Looking at me, he added, 'Here is your mother.' We understood. Our families had always been close; from this moment on, we would be one family. I put my arm round Mary. Her sobbing rose and fell in quiet waves of sorrow.

Then Mary Magdalene drew me aside for a moment. 'It's better if Mary doesn't stay too long.'

I looked blank.

'Remember, it's Friday with the Passover to come. They'll think about asking the Romans to break the legs of those on the crosses to get it all over before sunset. That's a horrible thing to watch.'

The sky had started to get dark and I felt she was right. The time had come. His mother had seen enough.

'Your son has told us what to do,' I whispered, 'and there is nothing else for us here. Let's return home where we can pray quietly and you will be safe.'

I feared she'd insist on staying but I think she'd seen as much horror as she could bear. She let me guide her away. As we walked slowly home, I couldn't help thinking how grand and wonderful the hope had been, and how horrific and dismal this ending was.

## Where to find this story in your Bible?

- Luke 23:25–44
- Matthew 27:36–43
- Mark 15:29–32
- John 19:25–27

# Finished:
## Mary Magdalene sees the end of it all

We got there at the beginning and stayed. It sounds like a boast but it isn't meant to be. Whatever I may have said, I didn't expect to survive the horrors of seeing his crucifixion. But I did.

Others, perhaps with more sense, came and went – there was nothing we could do. But I'd made my decision before I set out. I'd come to the foot of the cross and nothing would move me. To be honest, it's safer to be a woman in such a situation. It's accepted that we'll wail and it's assumed we're no political threat. That's exactly how unaware men can be.

Of course, we shed tears, but we also wanted to show Jesus that we were there for him. We couldn't do anything but we wouldn't desert him. Even when the sky grew black, we stayed.

The darkness was eerie: as if night had decided to replace day altogether. It must have lasted several hours or at least it seemed like that.

In the last throes of that darkness, Jesus cried out, 'Eloi, Eloi, lama sabachthani?'

It means, 'My God, my God, why have you forsaken me?'

I thought to myself, he's lost to us, he's gone to another place and he will never return. In all the bleak hopelessness, that was the hardest moment of all. Someone imagined he was crying out to a prophet and another one suggested it was Elijah. To me, it was just the sound of desolation.

Then he told us how thirsty he was and one of the bystanders ran to get a long stick with a sponge on it filled with wine vinegar in order that he could have something to drink in his suffering. To my horror, there were several who wanted him to hang there without any respite at all.

'No,' they yelled. 'Leave him to it and let's see if Elijah actually appears to save him.'

They were ignored and his lips were quenched at least a little. That tiny drink was his very last action. He committed his spirit back to his Father and said one final word. 'Finished.'

It could have been a cry of exhaustion, but it sounded more like the cry of a man who had crossed a finishing line. The thought didn't totally convince me. I wondered if I was simply imagining what I wanted to imagine.

Then there was a rumbling as if the earth itself was groaning. Rocks were dislodged and I'm told the curtain in the holiest part of the temple was torn right through. Earthquakes are not that unusual in Jerusalem but this one felt different. Even the Roman guards were shaken.

I heard one say to another, 'Surely, this was God's son.'

After the rumbling had subsided, most people left the scene but we stayed, watching from afar: the women who had been his team from the early days in Galilee and who still followed in spite of everything.

We would have been kinder to ourselves if we had left then. A messenger arrived from the barracks. He talked briefly to the centurion in charge who nodded.

They're going to break the prisoner's legs so they suffocate, I thought. And then the festival can continue without the inconvenient backdrop of an ongoing crucifixion.

I was right. They broke the legs of the man on the right. I thought Jesus would be next but they moved past him and dealt with the one on the left. It was swift and brutal.

Only then did they turn to Jesus. I wondered if they were slightly afraid of the man called the king. There was a brief discussion as if they were checking that Jesus had in fact died.

I thought to myself: at least they're not going to break his legs. And they didn't. I relaxed. But, as they turned to go, one of the soldiers thrust a spear into his side causing blood and water to pour out.

When Jesus had said 'Finished', I had been able to accept what had happened. Up to that point, I had found enough strength through being with him. Now, my final memory of the day would be that casual spear shoved thoughtlessly into his side just to check the obvious. Sometimes cruelty and sorrow seem to have no end at all.

## Where to find this story in your Bible?

- Matthew 27:46–56
- Mark 15:34–41
- Luke 23:45–49
- John 19:28–37

# This time:
## Joseph of Arimathea steps up

'We must do something,' Nicodemus declared with a mixture of determination and desperation in his voice.

It was not clear to me what he had in mind.

'We cannot leave him out there to be taken apart and eaten by the wolves,' he continued. 'Nor can we allow his bones to be picked clean by vultures.'

I bowed my head. I'd seen those sights all too often as I'd gone about my business around the city. We were intended to see such things. That was how Rome reminded us of its presence.

'It will require the permission of the procurator,' Nicodemus pointed out. 'Someone will need to see Pontius Pilate.'

'I will go,' I said before I'd had time to think about what I was saying.

'You?' said Nicodemus. 'Are you sure you want that job? Think of your reputation.'

Of course I didn't want to make the visit but there comes a moment when you can't keep quiet anymore. If you don't step forward, what have you got left? You're not living your life; you're letting it happen to you.

'I've met Pilate several times before,' I told Nicodemus, 'We've got on well enough during those brief meetings. I think he sees me as quiet and respectful so I never look like a threat.'

'It will ruin your reputation with the council in one stroke.'

'Probably so, but I can bear it. It's time someone stood up to Caiaphas. And I have a new tomb ready to be used so the matter of burial is resolved by it being me who goes to see him.'

Nicodemus looked at me closely. 'You're a braver man than you sometimes look.'

'Well, I don't feel it.'

And I still didn't feel it when I arrived at the palace compound that Herod the Great had built and in which Pilate always tucked himself away when he was obliged to visit the city.

He was not unduly surprised to see me but he was astonished by my request.

'I'd like to give Jesus of Nazareth a decent burial,' I told him. 'Our scriptures command us to bury a corpse that is hanging on a tree before the day is out.'

Pilate looked puzzled. The man who governed life and death in our land was totally confused by our religion even at the best of times. I understood that. He might have been in charge of the country but he was still a soldier at heart. And, as such, he found it very hard to believe that the death had occurred already. He summoned the centurion who had overseen the executions.

'Absolutely dead, sir,' he was told. 'Didn't even need to break his legs but we pierced his side with a spear just to make doubly sure.'

That was it. He released the body to me with a look of complete bafflement on his face. It was understandable. Firstly, some of the council come screaming for his blood. Then another wants to care for the dead body.

I expressed my gratitude for his willingness to allow a proper burial to take place and made my exit. Quite suddenly, I didn't feel afraid anymore. There was something that needed to be done and it fell to me this time.

I bought the necessary length of linen cloth on the way back from the palace to meet Nicodemus again. While I had been there, he had been ensuring we had the myrrh and aloes we would need.

Visiting Pilate was in some ways the easiest element of what we had to do. The worst part was collecting the body. The Romans know better than anyone how to make punishment effective. Every ounce of life had been drained or beaten out of his body.

His skin looked so pale, almost translucent in some places… a terrible ghostly version of who he had once been. Then there was the blood: so much of it, dark and congealed, staining his skin.

Part of me didn't want to touch the body at all. Another part of me wanted to wrap him in my arms, to say sorry and to make him come back to life. But he had been the miracle worker, not me.

We took him carefully from the cross, making sure that those terrible wounds where the nails had been driven in were not made even worse. As we trudged down the hill with his body, I remember thinking to myself: *What have they done to you, Jesus? How did we let it get this far out of control?*

It was a relief to get to my garden and to lay him in the tomb. We completed the burial requirements as best we could, then rolled a vast stone in front of the entrance.

When we'd done those things, I felt as satisfied as you ever can be in a moment like that. We had done everything which was possible in the ridiculously short period of time we had before the Sabbath and he was safe. Two of the Marys were with us and we all just stared in silence at the tomb for a minute or two.

The garden looked uncannily beautiful in the late sunshine. But he was dead and none of us could change that.

## Where to find this story in your Bible?

- Matthew 27:57–61
- Mark 15:42–47
- Luke 23:50–55
- John 19:38–42
- Deuteronomy 21:22–23

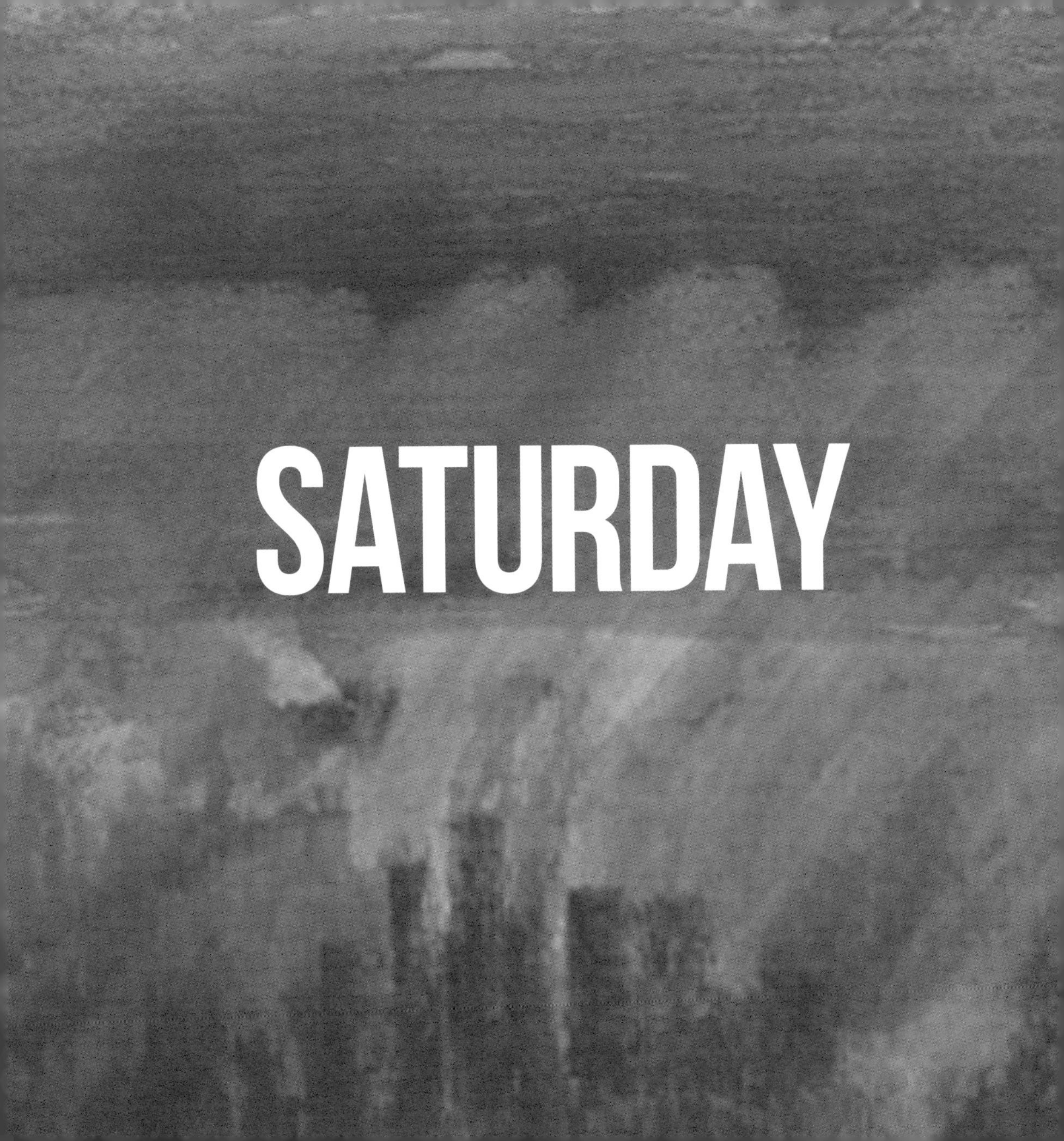
SATURDAY

# The dead stay dead:
## Caiaphas seals the tomb

It was once rumoured by an anonymous troublemaker that I was being paid too generously for the work I do as high priest. Let me tell you, no amount of money could recompense a man fully for the pressures that come with this post.

The moment Jesus had breathed his last you would have thought we were home and dry. Oh no. These matters are never over until you can be certain there are no loose ends, no chance whatsoever that the problem will not return in some form that's uglier than the last.

Once the body had been certified dead, I assumed the Romans would deal with it in some way. That was why I'd agreed with Pilate we needed this all over by sunset.

Well, it was indeed dealt with in one sense. A member of my council, of all people, requested the body for a proper burial and Pilate acceded to the request. I had no idea that such a quiet mouse of a man like Joseph of Arimathea had enough nerve in him. I'd never been entirely sure of his loyalty to me.

In theory, I should have been pleased – we knew where the body of this troublesome preacher had been put. The worrying question was whether it would stay there. It wasn't a problem I relished in the middle of our festival but it needed to be faced.

After a brief discussion with council members, it was decided that action must be taken. I told those with me how the Jewish law would be interpreted by us on this occasion. Should the question ever arise, I explained, executing our necessary priestly duties cannot conceivably be described as Sabbath-breaking.

Then we sent a message to Pilate and eventually gained an audience with him. I think it's fair to say that he was not pleased to see us.

'Your Excellency,' I began. 'We recall that, while he was still alive, the imposter who claimed to be our king alleged that he would rise again on the third day from death. If the disciples come and steal the body, they will start to claim that he has actually been raised from the tomb. The last lie will most certainly be worse than the first one.'

You could see in Pilate's eyes how disinterested he was in the proper concerns of keeping our people safe from false teaching. However, you could usually rely on him to take any route for a quiet life.

'Take a guard,' he said, without even looking up. Then he turned to me, 'It is your task to make the tomb as secure as you can.'

I got the message. He'd lend me the soldiers but the responsibility for the security was on our shoulders. That was fine by me. Once the tomb was sealed, we'd comfortably be able to deal with any hot-headed disciples. All that really mattered was that the dead stayed dead.

### Where to find this story in your Bible?

* Matthew 27:62–66

# A word in time:
## Joseph of Arimathea gets noticed

I went to the temple as I always did on the Sabbath but it wasn't the same. Where I had always been able to blend into the background, now the eyes of other people were upon me.

Some saw me and looked away; others hardened their features and looked bitterly at me. A few nodded as if they approved but did it briefly. I suspect that, overnight, it had become tricky, even dangerous to acknowledge me.

I'd gone from being one of the blandest bits of the establishment to beyond the pale in one small step. It had never occurred to me how fragile and fleeting some people's so-called friendship could be.

The one trouble with a Sabbath is that it's a day of rest, full stop. Much of the time that's exactly what I need. On this occasion, it gave me far too much time to go over and over the choices I hadn't made, the things I hadn't done, the words I hadn't said.

In the first place I need never have chosen to come to Jerusalem. I could have decided on a life in Arimathea. But I loved my academic work, was fascinated by the studies I'd pursued on the kingdom of God. Jerusalem was the very best place to follow my interests and to use my skills so, when the chance came, I took the opportunity.

Then there was the chance to be part of the Jewish Council. I was told I'd be mad to turn down the opportunity. Actually, I thought long and hard about doing just that. Eventually, I concluded that there was no real likelihood of me being in the limelight. Let other people do the politics, I told myself, just concentrate on interpreting the law with clarity and authority.

That worked well enough and, at times, they needed my skills and scriptural expertise. What they didn't want was my enthusiasm for the changes that their scriptures promised. God's word is only welcome, it seems, when it doesn't interfere with people's daily habits.

I'd first met Jesus when he was teaching in the temple. He brought fresh eyes to our history and our law. It excited me from the beginning. But almost from the start the chief priests had decided that this new preacher was a troublemaker so my contacts with him were secret affairs, managed under the cover of darkness.

Was Jesus the one who had been promised? Was he the one who would bring people back to faith and establish God's kingdom here on earth? It seemed a bit fanciful at first and frankly very unlikely that I should have been blessed by being born at such a time as that. But the more I heard him, the more confident I became.

My conviction about him made my silence at his trial all the more inexcusable. I'd always said that a word for the living is worth a thousand for the dead. It's no good waiting until a funeral to talk about the good things someone has done. But that was exactly how I'd behaved.

I walked around to see my friend Nicodemus for a while that afternoon and it helped a little to share my sorrow and shame with him. Then I talked with the two Marys about the spices and the perfumes for the completion of the burial. They were going to act as soon as the Sabbath was over. I told them I'd come across to talk with the guard if that was necessary.

Sorting out such details took my mind off what I could have done to ensure that this didn't happen in the first place. But nothing could keep me for long from the thought that I was mourning the dead when I might have been praising the living.

## Where to find this story in your Bible?

- Mark 15:42–43
- Luke 23:50–51, 56

# SUNDAY

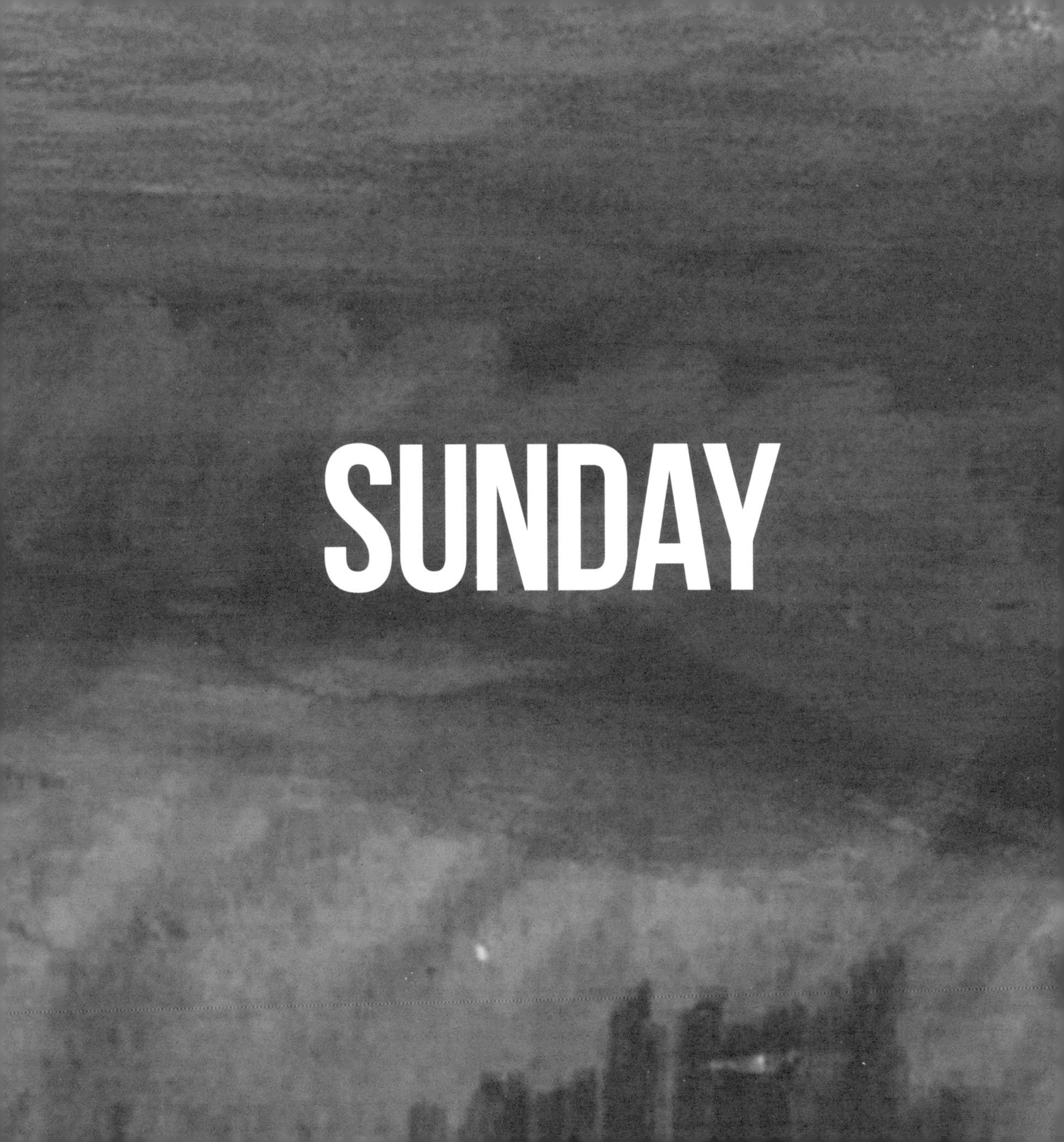

# The news gets through:
## Andrew in Bethany

When the Sabbath was over we felt we would have to do something. The problem was what it should be. Would going back to Jerusalem be the most dangerous and foolish thing we could do? Or was no one interested in us anymore? Were we in the firing line or could we shrink back into ordinary lives? Frankly we didn't know. But, as we sat eating bread together on that Sunday, there was a sound at the door.

*Friend or enemy* was the thought that flashed through my mind. I needn't have worried. It was John Mark.

'Glad to see you,' said Phillip. 'And relieved that you're safe.'

He looked down at his sandals. 'I didn't really understand the risk I was taking. I thought I'd be kept at home for weeks after Thursday night, but mum says I'm probably safer out of the city than in it. And I've told her I can do a man's work as well as most people. I'll officially be one when my next birthday comes around.'

'What the news?' I asked.

'It's quiet. That's what I've been sent to tell you. Peter and John have not been bothered by the authorities. They seem to have been satisfied with the work they've already done. And Jesus' body is safe in a garden tomb provided by Joseph of Arimathea who went to Pilate to request permission for a proper burial.'

I was astonished by that. 'So one of our most secret of secret followers has put himself in the spotlight?'

'That's right. Peter says Joseph's a bit stunned by all the sudden and disagreeable attention but he feels he can hold his head up now. If people hate him for what he's done, so be it. Nicodemus was his partner in the project so he's in deep water with the council as well.'

'Good on them both. And my brother? How is he?'

'Better when I saw him yesterday evening. I think it's because there are things to be done. The women were planning to meet at John's family house a little before daylight and go to the tomb to complete the burial duties. They should be there now.

'Caiaphas got Pilate to provide him with a Roman guard for the tomb. Apparently, he claimed he needed it to stop any disciples stealing the body. I don't think Pilate will have believed that for a second but it was a small price to pay for a peaceful Passover.'

'Will the guards let them into the tomb?'

'I don't think it will be an issue. Their job is to keep the body safe and having the women complete the proper rituals for burial seems pretty uncontroversial. They'll probably need some assistance from the soldiers because of the size of the stone rolled across the entrance. It's enormous, apparently.'

'So we are safe to return to the city?'

'Peter says you can never be sure but he thinks so. I'm here to invite you to meet up with him and John at our house later this morning. Actually, you've got to come because mum is baking bread and ordering fish at this very moment.'

'It sounds like a plan to me. At least we'll be together.'

'That's what Peter said. You can't bring the dead back to life but you can at least pray together and remember all they were to you.'

I looked at John Mark and suddenly felt so sorry for him. He was such a bright, intelligent boy, so ready to be helpful. And what had happened so far in his young life? He'd lost his dad; he'd lost the man he looked up to as a kind of second dad, and all this before he was even fully grown. At least we'd had three years on the road with Jesus. The boy deserved better than what had happened to him.

## Where to find this story in your Bible?

- Mark 14:50–51
- Matthew 27:57–61

# A goodbye:
## Joanna on burial duty

'I was not there to weep for him; I must be there to say goodbye to him.'

My husband nodded, 'You will not be needed in the palace this morning. Of course you can go with the other women. Indeed, you should go.'

So I left Herod's palace in the dark before the dawn, thinking of how, so often, I found myself stretched between two worlds. How much easier it would be if I didn't have responsibilities at court. But life isn't like that, is it? And perhaps I wouldn't understand other people's troubles if I didn't have my own to face.

At least on this day, the task ahead looked straightforward. I would meet up with Mary Magdalene and the others before it was fully light so we could make our way to the tomb without attracting attention.

Once there, we would ask the soldiers to open the tomb in order for us to complete the burial duties. When that was done, we would commit his body to God and thank the guards for their understanding. It would be a straightforward task and satisfying to have everything properly completed.

On my way to the house that John's family owned, I was sure I felt a rumble from deep in the earth. Tremors are common enough but it added to the strangeness I felt that morning. And, after the sound, there was an eerie silence, as if a breath was being held in.

When I arrived at the house, Mary Magdalene greeted me. She looked pale and drawn. That was no surprise after what had happened. Her attention was on the ointment and the spices for the morning's work.

'Everything must be in good order,' she told me, but it didn't sound convincing.

You can't put death right, can you? Our most careful and beautiful attention to detail wasn't going to turn back time. What we were dealing with wasn't the kind of pain which you could wrap your arms around like a mother does for a child when she whispers away the hurting.

Nonetheless, I understood how Mary felt. When you feel useless, the best medicine is to stay busy with small tasks. And, as soon as we were all gathered, we slipped out into the darkness.

I suppose it might have been sensible, as we walked along, to be quietly discussing what we were going to say to the soldiers. It was a delicate matter. They'd see half a dozen shadowy figures approaching before they realised who those people were. It would have been no surprise to be faced by guards with their swords drawn and ready for use.

As we walked in almost total silence, I kept going over the events in my mind: the Thursday night arrest, the botched trial process, the cross dragged to the place of execution. The fact that I had not been there meant my imagination was filling in the gaps and that wasn't good.

As we approached Joseph's garden, I breathed a sigh of relief. Now there was something to take my attention away from the events of the last few days.

Except there wasn't: not a soldier to be seen, only a stone rolled away. You'd have thought it was the earthquake we'd felt earlier except for the fact that things looked so tidy and untouched. Then we peered into the tomb. There was no body.

I was bewildered but Mary was horrified.

'Not this, surely not this,' she said.

I thought she was about to crumble into a heap but she didn't. Instead she covered her face with her hands for a moment, took a deep breath and looked up.

'Peter,' she said, as if she was suddenly determined. 'We need him here.'

And with that she turned and ran as if her life depended on it. And, in a sense, perhaps it did.

## Where to find this story in your Bible?

- Matthew 28:1
- Mark 16:1–4
- Luke 24:1–3
- John 20:1

# Not there:
## Mary Magdalene in a panic

I was halfway to John's house before it entered my brain that I'd left the other women by the tomb with no clear message about what they should do.

'Stupid,' I said to myself. 'You should have at least said something.'

But what was there to say? I had no idea.

Jerusalem is a city where grave-robbing has been a regular problem for years. Most of the time you don't think about it because you're getting on with your normal life. Then suddenly the danger hits you in the face and you realise that grave-robbing is not necessarily something that just happens to other people.

I felt sick to my stomach and I slowed to a halt. For a moment, I felt as if I couldn't go any further. There comes a time when you just want to give up, to lie down and curl up into a ball. But I knew I didn't have that choice.

'Lord, give me strength,' I said quietly and took several deep breaths. Then I did what I knew I had to do: I put one foot in front of the other and slowly picked up my pace until I was running so hard I thought my lungs were going to burst.

When I got to John's house, Peter opened the door and let me in. He stood there, looking puzzled, as he waited for me to get my breath. John joined him.

'Not there,' I gasped.

'What's not there?' asked John. 'Are we talking about the tomb?'

'Jesus isn't there.'

'He must be,' said Peter, 'unless you've gone to the wrong tomb.'

'I saw him laid to rest,' I reminded him. 'I was there. I know which garden belongs to Joseph of Arimathea.'

'Someone's moved the body,' suggested John. 'Joseph has a gardener. Perhaps it was him.'

'On a Sabbath?' asked Peter and scratched his head.

'You've got to come,' I told them. 'Once you've seen the garden, it will all make sense.'

Neither of them made any reply to that.

'It's not grave robbers, is it?' I asked. I hadn't dared say it until then.

Peter looked out of the door in the direction where the garden lay. 'There will be an explanation. The sooner we get there, the sooner we will have an answer.'

What he didn't say was whether it would be an answer we liked or not.

## Where to find this story in your Bible?

- John 20:2

# The young man:
## Joanna gets a message

The worst moments in life are those when you just don't know what to do. And, when Mary ran to get Peter, the rest of us stood there helplessly outside the tomb. Salome kept looking round as if she expected to find an answer, if only she could spot a clue as to what had happened.

What we didn't do was enter the tomb. We'd already peered in but that was it. *Why aren't we taking a proper look in there?* I asked myself.

Of course, we were scared of what we might find. Death is bad enough when you're facing it in plain daylight. In the shadows of a tomb not yet lit properly by the morning light, it becomes altogether more frightening.

I told myself that whatever was in there couldn't be any more terrifying than some of the things I'd seen in Herod's court so, with a quick prayer for protection from who knows what, I stepped forward. To my immense relief, the others followed.

We didn't get very far. To our total amazement, there was actually at least one young man dressed in white inside the tomb. I say 'at least' because the other Mary says she saw a second behind the first. To be honest, it was all too astonishing for me to take in properly.

As for the man I saw, he seemed to have been waiting for us. I must have looked more than a bit dazed and confused because the young man spoke very gently to me.

'Don't be alarmed,' he said, 'You're looking for Jesus of Nazareth, who was crucified, aren't you? He isn't here anymore; he has risen.'

Looking back, what he told us was perfectly clear, but it didn't seem that way in the half-light of the early morning. I think he must have sensed that.

'Take a look,' he told me. 'That was where he was laid.'

I could see what he meant. There were marks where the body had been and, beside them, the grave clothes, folded neatly. It may sound odd but I couldn't help thinking about how tidy it was. The neatness gave me hope. It didn't look like the end but rather a beginning and joy bubbled up inside of me.

The young man let me take my time, just waited so I could take it all in. There was something about him that made me think of angels. Perhaps it was how white his clothes were. I had assumed to begin with that he was simply a messenger. Then I realised that bringing messages was exactly what angels did. In my puzzlement, I stayed rooted to the spot.

He spoke again, 'This is the message you need to give to his followers. He is going on ahead of you to Galilee. You will see him there just as he promised you.'

Actually, I'm pretty sure he said more than that. It was about Jesus being handed over, about bad men being in charge for a while and about rising on the third day. There seemed to be so much to take in and frankly none of it related to what we had come to do that morning.

Instead there was a missing dead body, a tomb with strange beings in it and hard-to-believe messages we were supposed to carry. The joy I'd felt a moment earlier suddenly wasn't there. I was overwhelmed. It was simply more than I could cope with and I panicked. In fact, we all did. Not only did we turn and flee from the tomb, we left the garden altogether.

'Too much,' I kept saying to myself, 'way too much.' Halfway back down the road, we stopped because we realised that we had no idea what we were doing. Of course, we should have been going straight to where the disciples were due to meet that morning but we didn't. We were afraid. Afraid of what we'd seen and heard; frightened it might not be as real as we had thought when we were in the tomb; scared that we wouldn't be believed.

'Come back to my place?' I offered. 'We can have some breakfast; we can take stock. Perhaps we might even be able to make sense of what has happened to us.'

The first two of those three suggestions seemed eminently sensible: breakfast and taking stock. But making sense of the morning was something I wondered if we'd ever do.

## Where to find this story in your Bible?

- Mark 16:5–8
- Matthew 28:5–8a
- Luke 24:2–7

# The official line:
## Caiaphas bribes the guard

There are mornings when I wonder why I bother with other people. It would be so much simpler if I did everything myself. I don't expect to be loved; I don't even expect loyalty; I just think it's not too much to ask that people do their jobs.

The moment the guards arrived I knew there was another mess to deal with. Even the most inexperienced Roman soldier doesn't leave his post without good reason… or, in this case, bad reason.

The first thing I did was usher them into a private room. I knew before we even started I wasn't going to enjoy the meeting.

There was an earthquake, they said. That part of what they told me made sense – we all felt the tremor that morning. Then they talked about someone appearing from the heavens like a flash of lightning, rolling the tombstone away and terrorising them. That part made no sense at all.

I smelled their breath. No hint of cheap wine on it. Perhaps they'd been drugged, although I couldn't see how. Perhaps they'd been bribed by the disciples, although where that bunch could have rustled up enough money was a mystery to me.

I looked closely at the soldiers standing there. To my eyes, they were mere boys in uniform. Soldiers get younger every year around here. It seemed obvious to me that something strange had frightened them. For one dreadful moment, I wondered if they were telling me the truth. That was too terrible to contemplate so I set it aside.

The fact of the matter was clear: the body was missing. We needed to act. I sent for the other priests who listened to the story. Then, with the elders, we devised a plan.

I called the soldiers back in and offered them a large sum of money to say that the disciples had come during the night and stolen the body away.

The men look horrified.

'What if this story gets back to Pilate?' they asked. 'We could be dead men.'

'Our esteemed governor is not a man who hurries to judgement,' I told them. 'If the news gets back to him, I will explain the situation. I will also make clear our gratefulness for your role in keeping Jerusalem peaceful at this volatile time. He normally leaves very soon after the festival so what you fear is unlikely to happen. But you will be quite safe. Remember that the responsibility on this occasion has been placed on my shoulders. I am content to bear it.'

They thanked me for my selflessness and took the money. It really was an eye-watering sum. But needs must on some occasions. The last thing we wanted leaking out here was the truth… whatever that might actually be. The good news was that we had established an official line which would satisfy the majority of the population.

I dismissed the soldiers who were busily dividing up their reward. They thanked me and, as they left, I couldn't help but wonder what it was they had seen.

## Where to find this story in your Bible?

- Matthew 28:2–4, 11–15

# Not much to see:
## John runs to the tomb

We were sitting together doing not very much that Sunday morning. Peter had been asking me what I'd do after the burial duties were finished and the meeting with the other disciples had taken place.

I'd sighed rather heavily.

'What can we do?' I answered. 'I guess I'll go back to fishing. There's still a healthy business to be looked after. Instead of coming to Jerusalem with Jesus, I'll probably be coming with salt fish again. It's not a problem. This was my life until three years ago. I can fit back into it… I will miss him though.'

Peter nodded and said nothing. I understood. What can you say when things have fallen apart so completely?

Our conversation had ground to a halt by the time Mary Magdalene burst in with her news of a tomb without a body. I didn't like the sound of what Mary was describing one single bit.

I was about to ask her to go through what she'd seen again when Peter decided on action rather than discussion. 'The sooner we get back to the tomb,' he declared, 'the sooner we'll know.'

He was right. It was a puzzle that wasn't going to be solved by sitting and talking about it.

We set out for Joseph's garden and it quickly turned into a run. Mary had already rushed one way and Peter's older than me, so I comfortably outpaced them both.

As I got to the garden, I slowed. Suddenly it occurred to me that I could be going into the darkness of that tomb alone. Being ahead of the others no longer felt like such a good idea.

There's probably nothing to see, I told myself. But perhaps there was. A wild animal had got in and savaged the body. Some evil force had taken my master and was now waiting there for me. I know it sounds ridiculous, looking back, but it didn't at the time.

Peter's arrival saved me from making any decision about what to do. He just went straight past me and into the tomb. *That's why he's our leader*, I thought. And I followed.

There truly wasn't much to see. No wild animals, no strange apparitions, just the linen strips that had wrapped the body and the burial cloth for the head folded up by itself.

Mary arrived and stood there by our side as if to say 'I told you so'.

But what was this scene telling us? Peter looked long and hard at it all. I'm not quite sure what he thought at that moment. For me, I think it was the way the grave clothes were arranged that made the difference. Grave robbers don't fold linen like that. On the other hand, it was exactly how Jesus would have done it – neat, sensible, properly sorted. It seemed as if one chapter was over and another one had begun.

Standing there, I believed something was changing that morning, that we hadn't come to the end after all. A sense of hope began to grow inside of me, although quite what that feeling meant I had no idea just then. Peter said we should get back and we made to leave.

'I think I'll stay a little longer,' said Mary, 'if you don't mind.'

I smiled and nodded, 'You take as long as you like. You've done your bit for today.'

I don't think I've ever said anything that turned out to be more wrong.

### Where to find this story in your Bible?

- John 20:3–10

# Not believed:
## Joanna delivers the message

We sat around drinking cool water from the well, eating the very best olives you could find in Jerusalem and bread straight out of the royal ovens. It ought to have been delicious but, of course, it wasn't.

No matter how fine the food was, we were at a loss for what to do. It seemed so frustrating; I felt so useless. Firstly, I had been unable to give any help at all on the Friday. Now that I could be of some use, there was nothing for us to do except deliver an impossible message.

'We could tell one of my sons,' Salome suggested.

'But then we will have to tell the rest of the disciples,' Mary pointed out, 'and they will say we're out of our minds.'

'Perhaps, they'd be right,' I suggested. 'It could all have been some kind of collective hallucination.'

'Did it feel like that?' Salome asked. 'It seemed very real to me. I felt calm, almost joyful.'

Of course she was right. There was a sense of hope and joy where there should only have been sorrow. And we didn't panic at first. I had plenty of time to study what the young man had shown me.

The scene made sense when he let me look at it but something about his presence and his message then set off a kind of terror in me. I wasn't frightened of the young man himself; it was the whole experience that felt too much.

'They won't believe us,' I told the others, 'but Salome is right. This isn't a dream, a nightmare or a ghost story. It happened. And we aren't the only ones who have seen something.'

'What do you mean?' asked Mary.

'Would the soldiers have been overpowered by grave robbers?'

'Absolutely not.'

'So they saw something so astonishing, so terrifying in their eyes that they deserted their posts and ran. If it's all an illusion, it seems to have happened twice. That's even less likely than the story we've been given to tell.'

'But the guards won't admit that in public.'

'Probably not, but we can look out for some convenient lie being spread around. That will be proof enough for me that they've something to hide.'

And, on that basis, we set out to visit Mary, the mother of John Mark.

The disciples from Bethany had already arrived. And there were other followers too. John and Peter had also got there a few minutes before us. They were reporting on the empty tomb when we got there.

That should have made our task easier but arguably it had the opposite effect. If Peter hadn't seen a young man in white, how had we? If John had no story to tell of angels and messages, why did we have one?

It was clear that they thought our vivid imaginations had got the better of us and the terrors of the early morning had somehow been translated into crazy dreams. Looking back, I don't entirely blame them but it hurt a lot at the time. We were followers as much as they were and we deserved some respect. Instead we were treated as if what we had seen and heard was nonsense.

We didn't stay long. There was no purpose. Salome invited us back to her house to talk a little further. I didn't see how talking was going to help. Still, it gave us an excuse to depart.

If we weren't going to be believed, why on earth did that young man give us the message in the first place? The bits of the puzzle simply weren't fitting together.

Then I remembered what Chuza, my husband, used to say to me when Herod had landed him with some impossible situation or problem. 'It's not where we are at the moment that matters,' he'd say, 'it's where we finish up that counts.' I hoped with all my heart that proved to be true for us as well.

## Where to find this story in your Bible?

- Luke 24:8–11

# Back together:
## Andrew hears what has happened

We slipped back into Jerusalem and made our way with John Mark to Mary's house via the side streets and the alleyways. There was no point in drawing attention to ourselves. A few of the other followers of Jesus were already there. Peter and John arrived soon afterwards.

It was so good to see my brother again and I gave him a massive hug. There had been times when I feared I wouldn't see him again. But here he was: large as life and a free man.

'We have news,' he told us and his tone of voice suggested he wasn't entirely sure if it was good or bad. 'The tomb is empty.'

'That's not possible,' said Thomas.

'It's more than possible if grave robbers have been at their business,' muttered Simon Zealot.

'The grave was secured by a guard,' explained John. 'Caiaphas had got permission to deploy Roman soldiers to ensure that nothing untoward happened.'

'Yet it did,' observed Simon.

'True, but I'm not so sure about robbers. Mary Magdalene brought us the news and we went to investigate. Frankly, I didn't believe her at first. But she was right. The tomb is empty except for neatly folded grave clothes. No soldiers. No sign of any fight or struggle. It was almost as if it had never happened… or, if it had happened, it was now all over.'

There was a long pause as people looked at each other. It felt like everyone in the room was trying to make sense of what they had just heard. Either they couldn't do that or they didn't want to be the first to say something in case they looked stupid.

'Has he gone beyond death?' John asked us. 'You remember Lazarus and how he came out of the tomb when he was called by Jesus. Is it possible? I can't be sure but I believe it might be.'

Others were less convinced. James said his brother was always an optimist and Phillip said there could be several explanations of an empty tomb of which the simplest was that Joseph's gardener had moved the body somewhere safer.

Thomas asked John about what evidence had made him come to his conclusion. John shrugged: it was just a feeling. Matthew was able to recall something of what Jesus had said about being with us, being parted and in a little while seeing him again. We were racking our brains to remember exactly what Jesus had said when several of the women turned up.

They'd come to tell us not only about the empty tomb but about a young man in white with messages for them, someone they thought was an angel. It all sounded a bit fuzzy the way they were telling it.

'Let's get this clear,' said Thomas. 'You saw a man, possibly more than one, in dazzling white, who gave you messages for us.'

Joanna nodded.

'But neither Peter nor John saw anything.'

'They weren't with us. We'd left before they arrived.'

'You didn't think to stay and tell them what you'd seen and heard?'

'It was… we were… I don't know quite how to put it. Honestly, it was pretty frightening as well as exciting so we felt we couldn't stay in the garden. We probably shouldn't have been scared but we were. Well, I was, definitely. You'd need to ask the others if they felt it too.'

The other women nodded and Salome added, 'But we came as soon as we'd had time to gather ourselves. Remember how early we arose to complete the burial duties.'

I looked at the women who had joined us. To be honest, they looked as if they'd seen a ghost. I wanted to believe them, wanted to think that someday soon we'd meet Jesus again by the shores of Lake Galilee. But I couldn't. Something strange had happened to them. That much was clear. But the message they'd brought? That felt like wishful thinking.

## Where to find this story in your Bible?

- Luke 24:8–11

# His voice:
## Mary Magdalene is astonished

They left me alone. Sometimes that's all you want. Just to be able to breathe slowly and sort through the mess of things in your head. As Peter and John left Joseph's garden, I slumped to the ground, I couldn't remain standing any longer.

And I wept. Wept for all the hopes that had been torn away; wept for the loss of the one person who understood the whole of me; wept for all of us who had followed him, certain that he was the one who would make the difference.

The sorrow hit me in wave after wave. I'd be calming down and gathering myself a little when some other memory of him would be triggered and I'd feel totally bereft again.

How long this went on I have no idea but eventually the tide of misery ebbed away a bit and I looked around. It was such a beautiful garden. Joseph had designed it to be his oasis of peace. And it was just that: a quiet breathing space beyond the madness of the city.

I looked across at the tomb and felt my tears start again. It was so unfair that such a lovely place should be the centre of such a horrible loss. Getting up, I walked across to take another look. Not that it would do any good.

I expected the grave to be empty of course. This time, when I peered in, it was anything but. Where Jesus had been laid, there were two figures in white. It was almost as if they were guarding a body that wasn't there.

'Why are you crying?' they asked me.

I explained, 'They have taken my Lord away and I do not know where they have laid him.'

They didn't give me an answer so I turned around to see if I was missing something and found I wasn't alone in the garden. At last, I thought to myself, someone who will give me an answer. Without even thinking, I just assumed it was the gardener returned from his work of relocating the body.

He asked me, 'Why are crying? Who is it you are looking for?'

'Sir,' I answered, 'if you have taken him away, let me know me where you have put him and I will go and take care of him.'

If I hadn't been crying so much, I'd have taken a good look at the person I was talking to but I didn't. That changed with a single word.

'Mary,' he said.

Only one person called my name quite like that. And I opened my eyes properly at last.

'Master!' I gasped.

It was the one who had taught me everything: Jesus wasn't lost after all.

Or was he? I was in such a state I thought I must be dreaming. *It's all in the mind*, my fears started telling me. And the idea that this was a ghost went through my head even though I've always said I don't believe in them.

So I did the only thing I could do: I reached out and held him. To my immense relief and utter astonishment, there was someone to hold on to. I hadn't lost him. He had come back to me.

Of course, extraordinary moments cannot last forever. He told me very gently that I couldn't keep clinging to him, that he had to return to his Father. And he gave me a job to do.

'Go to my brothers and sisters and tell them: I am returning to my Father and your Father, to my God and your God.'

So I did. Instead of bringing a bundle of questions and doubts, as I had earlier, now I had good news to share. As for where Jesus went next, I simply can't tell you because, when I left him to do what he had asked of me, I never looked back.

## Where to find this story in your Bible?

- John 20:11–17

# A step too far:
## Matthew hears the stories

If you're a tax collector, you need your wits about you. In particular, you need to have a sense of when you're being told the truth and when someone is trying to hoodwink you.

So, on that Sunday morning, when the women arrived with a story that sounded like a vision of heavenly angels, I was watching with special care. Was it true? I was satisfied that they thought it was. Could it be true? That seemed very unlikely.

After they'd gone, we asked John a few more questions and then began to think about the consequences of an empty tomb for the rest of us. Bartholomew feared that it made the whole situation far more volatile, especially if stories started to do the rounds about messages from angels and Jesus not being dead after all.

I was about to suggest that we stay calm and take things one step at a time, when John Mark's mother, Mary, poked her head around the door. She explained that she'd just been to the market and had heard a rumour that the guards on the tomb were claiming that the disciples had stolen the body.

You didn't need to be a genius to guess where that lie had originated. Not with a few Roman soldiers. It could only be Caiaphas. My guess was that he was rattled and had paid off the guards to spread the story. Suddenly we were in danger. The fact that most of us were in Bethany when all this was supposed to have taken place wouldn't save us any more than the truth had helped Jesus.

'Bolt the door,' I said, rather abruptly.

Andrew, who was nearest, didn't need to be told twice.

'We need to warn the women about what is being said. It can only make it more dangerous for every one of us.'

'Could what they were telling us be true?' asked John. 'The tomb is empty and you don't spread a rumour like the one we've just heard if you believe nothing has really happened.'

'But it is nonsense,' insisted Thomas. 'It must be.'

He was right in a way. In any other situation, you'd quickly dismiss the story out of hand. But this wasn't any other situation any more than Jesus had been any other rabbi.

I wondered to myself whether we were dismissing the story simply because it came from the women among his disciples. If Jesus were actually to come back, I would have imagined him coming first to Peter or perhaps to the eleven of us. It's far too easy to dismiss things when you have a greater sense of your own status than you should.

I thought for a moment of all the times Jesus had changed our expectations about the way things should be. And, from my own experience, I knew that Caesar made no differences between men and women when it came to paying taxes.

All this was flowing through my brain when there was a knock on the door of the room.

'Who is it?' Peter demanded.

'Mary Magdalene,' was the reply and Philip let her in.

Where the other women had looked pale, she seemed flushed and excited.

'He's back, he's back!' she almost yelled. 'I've met him and I've been given a message.'

She paused.

'Go on,' John said. 'What's happened?'

'You're going to say it's nonsense.'

We felt a bit uncomfortable at that accusation.

'Have you been talking to the other women?' asked John.

'No, I've not seen them since I left the tomb to find you and Peter.'

'But you have seen something.'

Mary nodded, 'I stayed after you left because I wanted a quiet place where I could grieve. It's a lovely garden, a perfect place for sorrows. But you can't just cry forever, and my curiosity got the better of me. I peered into the tomb.'

She stopped.

'Go on,' Peter encouraged her.

'Well, there was no one in there when you left, was there?'

Peter nodded.

'So I didn't expect to see anyone. I just wanted to look quietly at where Jesus had been. The body still wasn't there but two people were. It was as if they'd been waiting for me.'

'How were they dressed?' asked Andrew.

'In white,' she explained, 'and there was a brightness like you imagine angels to have. But I wasn't particularly thinking about that at the time. All I wanted to know was where Jesus was. They didn't actually tell me that, simply asked why I was crying. I told them about Jesus but, because they didn't say any more, I turned back to the garden as I'd heard a slight rustling.'

'And was there anything?' asked John.

'A man had appeared. I just assumed he was the gardener so I asked him where he had put the body. It was all fitting into place… or so I thought. Then he called my name: Mary. And I knew it was Jesus.'

'But you might not have been sure,' Thomas pointed out.

'You're right,' she said. 'The moment I was clear that it was our master, I doubted myself again. What if it was a trick of the light, a dream? I've never believed in ghosts but…'

'So you can't be sure,' said John, very gently.

'Actually, I can. I said a very quick prayer and put my arms around whatever was in front of me. I don't think I've ever been so scared in my life. But he was there – I held him so I know. It was the most wonderful thing that has ever happened to me. Then he explained I couldn't just go on clinging to him because he had to return to his Father and our Father, his God and our God. That was the message for you. And that's why I've come straight here. Surely, you're going to see him too.'

We all looked around at one another and this time nobody said 'nonsense'. There was too much detail in what Mary had said to dismiss it. And some of that detail had echoes of what we had heard earlier.

But what stopped me in my tracks was the tangible evidence. She said she had held him. Of course it could still have been imagination but it simply didn't sound like a ghost story.

Mary sat down as if exhausted by her storytelling and John Mark went off to get a jug of water and another cup.

'What happens next?' asked Andrew.

'We wait and see. If Mary is right, it will become clear to all of us,' his brother replied.

Thomas made the sort of noise that suggested he wasn't convinced in the slightest and I think he was going to say something but the other women returned in great excitement before he could get going.

They told us they were on the way to Salome's place when Jesus greeted them, saying 'Shalom', encouraging them not to be afraid and telling them that he would meet us in Galilee. And, yes, they had physically held him too.

It didn't have the detail of Mary Magdalene's story but the accounts seemed to me to fit together. To be honest, I don't think I quite believed what I'd heard, and I'm certain Thomas didn't. On the other hand it was clear that something strange was happening. Could our master, who had died in full view of so many people, have actually returned? At that moment, it seemed all too chaotic and confusing. For me, it was the thing you want to believe but can't.

## Where to find this story in your Bible?

- John 20:18
- Matthew 28:9–10

# The puzzle:
## Mary, wife of Cleopas, on listening

We were well into the day by the time Mary Magdalene and the other women had told their stories. Matthew was scratching his head and Thomas had that 'everything is nonsense' look on his face. It appeared whenever he couldn't work something out. As for my husband, he'd decided to walk with his cousin Reuben back to Emmaus.

I wasn't surprised and wished them both a good journey. They certainly wouldn't be able to dawdle if they wanted to get there by nightfall. It could have been left a day or two but Cleopas had told our daughter to expect him, God willing, on the day after the Sabbath. She wouldn't have worried if we all stayed a few days longer in the city – she's perfectly competent to manage the household without either of us. In fact, I think she rather likes it. But my husband prefers his own bed and his own surroundings.

You can't blame him. Emmaus is a lovely place. And, on this occasion, I think he wanted to get away from empty tombs, angel voices and messages that people were claiming came from Jesus.

As one of those who had brought the news, I was thoroughly fed up with the fact that we hadn't been believed. Of course, it was prejudice against women. I thought so anyway. Jesus had treated everyone the same. You couldn't always say that about his followers.

It was good of his cousin to make the journey with him. I suspected he wanted a quiet open road in order to chew over what had happened as much as my husband did. Knowing both of them, I assumed they'd be going through the story detail by detail, from beginning to end, in order to search out some clue, any clue that would help make sense of what had happened.

What no one expected was that we'd see them again that evening. It was late and some of the disciples including Peter had left. I think it was for a time of prayer. When Cleopas and Reuben first arrived, flushed and flustered, I feared they'd been robbed somewhere on their journey.

It wasn't that at all. They had fallen into conversation with someone along the road. They hadn't taken too much notice of their fellow-traveller initially. The thing that surprised them both was that he didn't seem to know the Jesus story at all.

'What!' my husband had exclaimed. 'Are you the only one in Jerusalem who hasn't heard what's happened during the last few days?'

That's Cleopas for you: blunt to the point of awkwardness. But, to be fair, he filled the stranger in on what had happened pretty comprehensively: our hopes, our fears, his crucifixion, plus the confusing business of the empty tomb and what we had told them. Instead of just taking it all in, the stranger began to give his slant on the events – clearly he did know what had been going on after all.

'He called us dim-witted and slow to believe!' Cleopas complained.

I smiled; didn't say anything.

'He started right back at Moses and the way he explained it made everything clear. We arrived in Emmaus as the sun was sinking and I insisted he stayed to eat. Because he was our guest, I asked him to bless the meal. He took the bread, broke it and gave it to us. Suddenly I knew it was Jesus and wondered why I hadn't seen it before. Then he disappeared.'

I thought to myself: that's a worse ending to a story than ours was. But it had clearly energised them and they told us how it had felt as if they were on fire when he explained it all.

It was then that I realised how difficult it was to get across strange and unexpected things, however wonderful they might be. One look around the room was enough for me to realise it was not only us who were doubted on this day of revelations. But, on this occasion, the doubt lasted no longer than it took for the door to open.

'You'll never guess what's happened!' yelled Phillip.

That seemed entirely probable.

'Peter has met Jesus.'

'And I didn't even want to,' Peter admitted uncomfortably, 'after what I'd said and done. But he is risen, he's here again and you will meet him.'

It felt like the last piece of the puzzle had been given to us. Suddenly, there were apologies for what had been said earlier and lots of hugs. After that, Cleopas had to tell his story all over again, which, being Cleopas, he rather liked.

### Where to find this story in your Bible?

- Mark 16:12–13
- Luke 24:13–32

# A bite to eat:
## Andrew sees as well as hears

The appearance of Jesus to my brother was, in theory, the perfect way to round off an utterly remarkable day. The evidence fitted together; there were multiple witnesses and several instances.

It ought to have been enough evidence for anyone. Yet it didn't totally satisfy me. I couldn't work it out at first; felt embarrassed about my lingering doubt so kept my mouth firmly shut.

As it was getting late, people began to depart to their own houses and beds, leaving just a core of us still talking with Cleopas about what had happened on the Emmaus Road. After Thomas had left with Bartimaeus and I'd bolted the door again for safety, a thought struck me.

Bartimaeus! I'd never understood how important seeing was until he joined our group. You take such things for granted. And that was what I needed. I didn't just want Peter to tell me Jesus was back, I hungered to see him for myself.

Be careful what you wish for. It might happen. We were still going over the day's events and discussing what it might mean for us, when I heard a voice.

'Shalom.'

It was my Mary Magdalene moment. Suddenly I knew what she meant about knowing Jesus when he greeted you. But the door was locked. I knew that for certain because I'd done it.

So what I was hearing wasn't possible. I turned, as we all did, to where the voice was coming from.

It looked like Jesus; it sounded like Jesus, but was it him? I'd often heard about the tricks that the mind can play when you're out in the desert.

Or perhaps it was a ghost? I think that was the first thought most of us had. I can't speak for the others but I, for one, was terrified.

He asked us why we were so startled and scared, why we were jumping straight to questions and doubts.

'Look at me,' he commanded. 'My hands and feet.'

I winced as I saw the wounds.

'It really is me. Touch me and see. A ghost doesn't have flesh and bones.'

Then he told us off for our lack of faith. It wasn't unkindly but it was definitely a fair comment. After all, if we didn't believe, who on earth would? It reminded me of all those times I'd been dismissive of others and I silently promised God I'd do better in the future.

In spite of him actually being there, Jesus could see that not all of us were totally convinced. We were thrilled, we were amazed, but I don't think we could quite take it in.

He paused, looked around at us and smiled slightly, 'Have you got anything here to eat?'

He asked it as if he'd actually just dropped in for snack. Well, we did have something as it happened: a piece of broiled fish left over from supper. We gave it to him and watched in amazement as he ate.

He explained things to us as he had to Cleopas on the road to Emmaus. I began to feel I understood properly for the first time what he had been saying all along. Even more importantly he said that as he had been sent by God, so now he was sending us out with his Spirit. We felt it too, like a breath filling us.

He said it would be up to us to bring God's forgiveness to people. Without us, it wouldn't happen. That felt jaw-dropping. And I've never forgotten it in all the years since. But the thing I tell people first about that evening is the easiest bit to understand: dead men don't eat fish.

## Where to find this story in your Bible?

- Mark 16:14
- Luke 24:36–44
- John 20:19–23

# LATER

# Doubt:
## Matthew anticipates a problem

When I realised who wasn't there late on the Sunday evening as Jesus ate fish with us, I knew fairly clearly what would happen the next morning.

I had found what Jesus had done astonishing even though I was there. Thomas, the one of us who always asked for the evidence, was going to find it both unbelievable and ridiculous.

'We've seen the Lord,' said James, the next morning as soon as Thomas was back with us. He then went into a slightly garbled account of what had happened. Not that I think I'd have expressed it any better.

Thomas waited patiently, hands on hips. When James finished, Thomas looked long and hard at his friend.

'No,' he told him.

Some of the others who were there weighed in to support what James had been saying. I didn't. I could see it was making the situation worse.

Eventually, Thomas almost exploded. 'Unless I see the nail marks in his hands,' he told James, 'I will not believe.'

Looking round at all of us, he continued, 'Unless I can actually put my fingers where the nails were and my hand into his side, I will never believe.'

Nobody said much after that. Some made their excuses in order to run minor errands and eventually Thomas himself said he was stepping out to get some fresh air.

It was a strange week after that. I'd assumed Jesus would come back most days and spend some time with us, but he didn't. The longer that went on the more I began to doubt what I'd seen with my own eyes.

And my heart went out to Thomas. His anger subsided soon enough, only to be replaced by a dark loneliness. He didn't believe us, he couldn't believe us, but he didn't know what to believe in its place. Nothing, I suppose. It was tough for him.

But I give Thomas a lot of credit, too. He didn't walk away; he didn't pour more scorn on us. When there were prayer times he joined in; when we listened to scripture in the temple, he listened along with us. What he was thinking, I have no idea. But he didn't give up or give in.

Then it happened. It was the next Sunday, quite late. The doors were locked as they always were that week. Suddenly, there was that greeting again, 'Shalom.' From nowhere, Jesus was in the midst of us. I was standing right by Thomas when this happened. He went absolutely rigid. I thought, for a moment, that he'd had a fit.

Jesus turned and looked at him. 'Put your finger here, Thomas,' he commanded. 'Look at my hands. Reach out your own hand and put it in my side. Stop doubting and believe.'

None of us did or said anything.

I wondered if Thomas was about to apologise for being so cross last week or explain to Jesus about how it had sounded frankly ridiculous the way we'd tried to explain what had happened.

Instead, Thomas eventually took the deepest of deep breaths and said, 'My Lord… and my God.'

'That's it,' I thought to myself. Thomas is right. We're not just standing in the presence of the one we have followed; we're standing in the presence of the one who was promised centuries ago: Son of Man, Son of God.

And while all this was racing through my head, Jesus turned again to Thomas.

'You believe because you have seen me,' he observed. 'Just think what a blessing, what a joy it is and will be for those who have not seen this and yet still can believe.'

That was the moment I knew a new era was opening. What we were seeing, hearing, touching was only a start. Some days we had probably got a little too fond of our place in the story but actually we were only the beginning.

## Where to find this story in your Bible?

- John 20:24–29

# Farewell to the city:
## Mary Magdalene heads north

It was the Monday after the evening Jesus appeared to Thomas and I was sitting with Peter in the courtyard of John Mark's house.

So much had happened in that home. The last meal together that I'd helped the disciples to prepare still haunted Peter and I watched him as I looked up towards the room where it had happened.

It seemed like the right moment to talk about the future and what might happen next.

'I'm going back to Galilee for a while,' I told him.

He smiled and nodded.

'Salome, James and John want to come as well. We're going to stay over in Bethany with Mary and Martha tonight so we can all catch up. Then we'll start the trek in earnest tomorrow morning.'

'It's a good idea,' he told me. 'If the four of you lead the way, we can follow over the next few days. It may be safer to be spread out like that.'

'I feel confined in the city,' I told him. 'The threat never quite recedes. I've seen so many bad things here.'

'And wonders, too,' he reminded me.

'Wonders I thought I'd never see,' I agreed. 'But I'll still breathe a whole lot easier by the lake.'

Before I left, Peter came to find me. It was unexpected and I didn't quite know what he wanted.

'Coming to to say you'll miss me?' I asked and then laughed to cover my uncertainty.

He smiled, 'Well, yes. But also, there are things I've said in the past few weeks that I shouldn't have and other things I should have said but didn't. One is telling you how important you've been in all this. I've not been much of a rock but you've been an absolute tower. If anyone deserves their nickname, you do. Your strength has put the rest of us to shame.'

'I only do my bit.'

'But what a bit that is. And you were the one who brought us the most important news, even if we weren't ready to hear it properly.'

'Why on earth did he choose me for that?'

'Perhaps because he could trust you to bring the message whether or not anyone believed it. He knew you wouldn't hide away and keep what had happened a secret. And he was right. So thank you.'

That was the kindest and best send-off I've ever had.

As I was leaving to meet up with Salome and family, I turned back for a moment.

Peter grinned, 'I know what you're thinking. Will the rest actually come back to Galilee as well? Of course we will.'

## Where to find this story in your Bible?

- Matthew 28:10
- Mark 16:7

# Breakfast on the shore:
## Simon Peter goes fishing

The air smelled sweet. You forget that when you've been away. It was so, so good to be back in Galilee after the posturing and positioning of the city. Back in Capernaum, there's no need to keep examining your words. You're with regular people so you can just say it like it is.

Except that, this time, when people asked what had been happening, I started to talk about a man who had died and was alive again. Not a healing but a resurrection.

People who knew about Jesus, and most did, would then ask: well, where is he? And I'd say I'm not sure. Then I'd try to explain how he just turns up out of nowhere from time to time.

'Does he knock?' they'd ask and I'd have to admit that he sort of appears, sometimes through walls.

The person who proved to be most persistent in his questioning was Benjamin, my young nephew, who had started on the boats while I was away.

'Sounds a bit weird to me, uncle, but you're the boss.'

That gave me a rare moment of laughter. 'So bosses can be as mad as they like! Is that what you're saying?'

'Not mad, just weird. Me and my friends like weird. There's too much dull and normal around here. And, anyway, just because it's weird doesn't mean it's wrong.'

He's a tonic, Benjamin; has been since he was little. What I didn't mention to him was how ambiguous I felt about Jesus reappearing. I knew well enough how strange that Thursday night and Friday morning had been for all of us. But it still didn't excuse my disloyalty. I knew he'd forgiven me, put it in the past but I wasn't at all sure I had.

I didn't do any work on the boats in the first days after we got back but I soon found I missed it. One clear, still evening, I couldn't wait any longer.

'Who's up for a bit of night-fishing?' I asked.

Thomas, James, John and Nathanael joined me and a couple of others as well. It was an absolute treat to be out on the lake again in the cool of the evening.

However, as the night wore on without a sign of even a single fish, I began to think that someone or something was conspiring against me. Perhaps I didn't deserve to be a fisherman anymore. A silly thought, I know, but that's how it is when the darkness descends on you.

It was a relief when dawn began to break. We were not far out from the shore and, in the low rays of the early morning sun, we saw the outline of a figure on the water's edge.

'Not caught anything, lads?' a male voice called out.

'Not a single thing,' we shouted back.

'Try the other side. There's fish on the right hand – cast your net there.'

A pair of eyes from the shore is always useful – I'd been teaching Benjamin about that the other day. So we cast again and this time we simply couldn't believe it. There were so many fish we couldn't even begin to pull the net back into the boat.

As the sun continued to rise, John squinted again at the figure on the beach. His jaw dropped. 'It's the Lord,' he said.

I didn't wait to check if he was right. Grabbing something to wear, I jumped into the water and went to see him with the others bringing the boat and the net to shore with our bumper catch. It felt like we'd caught every fish in the sea. Not only that, I didn't spot a single tear in the net. Miraculous!

There was a charcoal fire and some bread ready for us. How this happened I have no idea. And Benjamin was there as well – come out early to see if he could help.

I got to shore ahead of the others but then it occurred to me that I had no idea what I wanted to say to Jesus.

Nor was I the only one. We all just stood there open-mouthed. Jesus broke the silence. 'Bring on over some of that fish you've caught,' he requested as if he did this sort of thing every day.

So we did. And we cooked breakfast together. While it was happening, I was thinking to myself: *I'm going to remember this meal just as much as that Passover supper.* And I always did. They went with one another.

Of course, we wanted to say things like 'Is it really you?' But we didn't. Benjamin came and sat beside me to eat, then went across to help with the nets. I can't quite explain why we said so little. I think it was because we were afraid he'd disappear as quickly as he'd appeared.

He didn't. Instead, after the meal, Jesus came across and joined me. We sat there together, looking at the boats pulled up against the shore. It felt like a perfect scene set out in front of us.

'Do you love me more than these?' he asked.

I wasn't quite sure what he meant. I do love boats. And I love the peace you feel when you're on the water looking for the right place and the right moment. But I don't love that more than him so the answer was the easiest 'yes' in the world.

Perhaps I'd said it too glibly because he pushed me then about how far I would actually go for him, asked me not once but twice more. What if the sacrifice wasn't about boats and fishing? What if my whole life was on the line? Not someone else's. Mine. It was the toughest talk I've ever had with anyone.

'Lord,' I told him, 'you know everything. You know how much I love you.'

He nodded and I realised that he wasn't asking because he didn't know; he was asking so I could be sure of it myself. I shed a quiet tear or two as I sat with him that morning but I felt the better for it. I knew I would follow him this time as far as the road took us, whatever the ending might be.

Of course, I wanted to know what it might mean for my friends as well but we weren't there to talk about that. I'd learnt what I needed to know about myself and that was enough.

'Did you learn much?' I asked Benjamin, later in the day when he was helping with the cleaning of the boats.

'Loads, uncle; it was great.'

'And exactly how did you get to meet Jesus by the lake?'

'Well, I'd come out to see if I could spot shoals of fish in the early sun like you explained and I wasn't doing very well at it. I was absolutely sure I was on my own and then suddenly he was there, too. Weird.'

'Yes, it is,' I admitted.

He agreed, 'But wonderful, too.'

And that is what is so important to hold on to as you get older: just because it's weird doesn't mean it's not wonderful as well.

## Where to find this story in your Bible?

- John 21:1–22

# The road ahead:
## Bartimaeus contemplates the future

After Jesus returned, I wondered where someone like me would fit in. During the days around the Passover, I'd found plenty of opportunities to make myself useful. I wasn't known in Jerusalem; I could help out, run errands, take messages and no one would challenge me. It felt special to be part of a team where my small advantages in a situation could be useful.

After Jesus returned and the initial fear of reprisals began to ebb away, I wondered whether I ought to take a step back and return to Jericho. Jesus didn't really need someone like me when there was a tight-knit inner group to look after matters.

Martha and Mary told me that was nonsense and I'd be useful to them for as long as I was still breathing. It was a kind thought but I wondered if they'd say that to whoever was with them.

What weighed more heavily in the scales when I was making up my mind was the look of horror on the face of John Mark's mother, Mary.

'Don't do that,' she begged me when she heard I was thinking of returning to Jericho. 'Mark is only just getting to know you. No one can replace his dad but he looks up to you in the way he did to him. You've experienced so much and he knows you'll always tell him things straight. He's actually been trying to write a short account of what you've told him about your life. Don't leave us now. Please.'

So I stayed. I heard the accounts of people meeting Jesus again and, to my astonishment became one of them. That truly wasn't such a rare event. If you ever get the idea that he just appeared to a few people, you need to dismiss the thought straight away. There were plenty of occasions and hundreds of witnesses.

And he didn't just appear; he spoke about what had occurred and what would happen next.

'You are my witnesses,' he'd declare, 'to every people.'

The message could hardly have been simpler: turn around; let God put the past behind you and experience what it is like to be forgiven.

'You are my hands and heart,' he'd say. 'You are my voices. And you will carry my Spirit in the very depths of your being as I have promised you.'

'That's just such a wonderful thing for Peter and the team to be called to do,' I told Mary Magdalene when we were talking together one evening.

'No,' she told me. 'That's not the point at all, Bartimaeus.'

She looked at me long and hard as if she was deciding whether I was looking for an excuse of really didn't understand.

'This is what he's calling all of us to do,' she continued. 'To get going, he needed a small team as a core but it was only ever a start. And even that core needed our support group. It's what makes Jesus unique. Everyone is welcome and nobody is going to ask about whether you're qualified enough. Being willing to come along is qualification enough.'

I wasn't fully convinced but I also heard Peter say much the same thing.

'We go everywhere,' he declared. 'Teach everyone; baptise whoever asks. Jesus will be with us for as long as we have breath. And how many of us does he need? All of us.'

Mary Magdalene was sitting next to me, when Peter was saying that. She nudged me in the ribs, 'told you,' she said quietly. 'We've gone from being players in the story to actually being the storytellers.'

### Where to find this story in your Bible?

- Matthew 28:18–20
- Luke 24:45–49
- 1 Corinthians 15:5–7

# No boundaries:
## Mary Magdalene, some years later

Galilee again and I'm looking out across the lake. It was still until a minute ago but the wind is stirring as it often does at this time of day. This is where I belonged before I met him – home to the discoveries and the troubles of my younger years.

Jesus swept all that away. I started again, couldn't believe my luck; didn't understand why he'd ever want me as part of his team. But he did. Of course, I started out wondering what his angle was but that was the astonishment – there was no angle. You were accepted for who you were.

It was hard at first when he was no longer here in person to turn to for advice and strength but I've discovered that it doesn't matter. We've learnt to pray more, listen better, put into practice what he told us to say. It works.

So, at long last, the road brings me back here again… for the moment, at least. Peter leads us, as Jesus had said he would. And he does it with the sort of tact and skill you might not have expected from a fisherman, even one who speaks three languages fluently. He declares we're a gathering of whoever will hear. That's brilliant! It's as if there are no boundaries anymore.

I still miss Jesus: the warmth of his voice, the sense that he knew what each and every one of us needed. But, when you find yourself where you are meant to be, everything seems to slot into place. I belong to him even more than I do to this lake. And that is all that matters.

As I look across at the eastern hills, I think of how different I am to the young girl who stood here all those years ago.

Back in the garden, when I held the man I thought I'd lost forever, he gave me a message: tell the others. That's what I did, what I still do whenever I have the chance. It's joyous to be back by the lake but I don't belong here as I once did.

There are roads to walk, people to meet, stories to tell. The wind stirs on the lake just as the breath of God does when you least expect it. I miss my Lord, sometimes terribly, but I know now we are never alone.

## Where to find this story in your Bible?

- Luke 8:1–3
- Acts 10:1–43

# Afterword:
## A conversation with David Kitchen

**What made you want to approach Easter in this way?**

Basically because I wanted to test the story. Was there enough evidence and information to put together an account that would make you feel as if you were there? I wasn't sure before I started.

It mattered, you see, because I'd grown up with friends who'd walked away from faith due to their doubts about Easter. Not all that surprising really. The claims made in the accounts seem frankly unbelievable. The dead are alive again? Who on earth has seen any evidence of that in Potter's Bar or Cheddleton?

But I disagreed with my friends' scepticism; I thought there was something in the accounts that rang true. And it helped me to find my faith. One of the big challenges is that we have four accounts written by different people for different reasons. That's a big plus in my view but it would be very strange if those accounts always fitted easily together.

**Did you ever actually feel the same way as your sceptical friends?**

Absolutely. It's natural to have doubts. In fact, it's a reassuring sign that we're normal! But it doesn't mean the doubts are right. A number of things have happened to me across the years that looked unbelievable at the time. So I have never been too shocked by strange events.

The question for me was whether the Easter story was one strange event too far or actually believable in spite of seeming to be the opposite. Was it possible for the range of accounts to tell a story in a way that made good sense however much it seemed to break the rules of life as we normally know it?

**And is that why you chose to tell the story through witnesses?**

Well, I'd always told the story of Mary Magdalene at the tomb through her eyes. It's such an extraordinary scene that it deserves to be brought alive. And later I wrote up Joseph of Arimathea's story for a BBC programme. But I'd never tried to recount the whole of Easter in that way.

**You've chosen a varied cast of characters for this retelling. How did you choose them?**

Mainly, they chose themselves. I'd already written an account of Palm Sunday through one of the disciple's eyes years ago. Then one day I wondered what the Palm Sunday crowd might have looked like from a Roman soldier's point of view. Suddenly, I felt as if I had a much fuller picture.

**You chose some people who are not named Bible characters. Why?**

I thought it was important that you had the chance to look at the story from a wide range of angles. The Jewish authorities make it very clear that the Romans are there watching when they tell Jesus to get his followers to pipe down on Palm Sunday. The watchtowers around Jerusalem weren't built for decoration; they were there to defend the city. Once I'd named my Roman soldiers and got them in place, scenes started to emerge.

And with the disciples who speak through this story, I wanted to get a sense of the range of people who followed Jesus. So there's Simon Peter as the leader, but there's also Simon Zealot, the nationalist and Matthew who, as a tax collector, had been a Roman collaborator. His followers sometimes seem like they've been assembled to see if the most diverse group of people possible can, in fact, become a team.

**Some of the characters through which the story is told are the obvious ones like Simon Peter but others are a surprise. I'd say that Bartimaeus is one of those.**

Yes, he sort of crept up on me. The gospels make clear that he follows Jesus from Jericho where he'd been healed so I had him in my mind when they arrive in Bethany. But once he'd arrived there, I had to decide what would have happened to him.

There are actually some clues in the gospels. Matthew, Mark and Luke all tell the story of the noisy beggar who Jesus heals by the Jericho gates. But it's Mark who provides his name and the fact that he leaves his big cloak behind. For some reason, those details matter to John Mark. The simple explanation would be that he knows the man which suggests Bartimaeus stays at least for a period of time in Jerusalem.

There's an important point in letting Bartimaeus play a role in the storytelling. He offers a reminder that there was a wider group of followers beyond the twelve. When he's describing what happens, we're looking from outside the inner circle of the closest and best-known followers. I've never felt as if I was part of some very select group, just one of the countless numbers that have followed across the centuries. So, in a funny sort of way, I can draw a direct line between Bartimaeus and myself in the here and now. His existence encourages me.

**He's not the only slightly unexpected character.**

True. Take Claudia Procula, who was Pilate's wife. She's critical to the way that the trial plays out so plays a brief but vital part in the story. And Joanna is one of the women whose role gets underplayed. She's our only link to the events in Herod's court. I've tried not to use too many characters to tell the story but enough to have that full range of perspectives.

**There were one or two other surprises for me. Why on earth do you imagine that John the disciple also delivered salt fish to Caiaphas?**

It's a fair question. The text tells us that John is known well enough in Jerusalem to gain access to the courtyard of Caiaphas, the high priest, on the night of Jesus' arrest. In fact, he's trusted enough to be able to gain entrance to the courtyard for Simon Peter too.

This raises the question of why he's known and there's an obvious, fairly simple answer. Salt fish was an important commodity traded between countryside and city. Zebedee, with his sons James and John had a fishing business.

It seems utterly reasonable to suggest that John, the younger son, might be part of their trading arrangements with the city. Indeed, tradition assigns Zebedee's name to a small house in Jerusalem. It's unlikely to be original but it's an indication that other people made a similar assumption long before I did.

**I can see why you called the book *Easter Inside Out* because it's such a thorough look at the story from the points of view of those who were there. Was it always going to be called that?**

Not at the start. I collect title ideas as I go along. First of all it was *All That Matters* because I was desperately keen not to exclude any part of the story that makes a difference to the whole narrative. Then it was *Dead Men Don't Eat Fish* which is a bit quirky but faces up to the fact that the resurrection is tough to believe even for the closest disciples. Later on, it became *Easter Astonished*.

**I like that. It's a story with so many unexpected twists and turns, isn't it?**

I couldn't agree more: the characters in this story feel excited, fearful, puzzled, frustrated and confused. But arguably most of all they feel astonished. Almost everything Jesus does from the start of the Palm Sunday walk creates astonishment in someone. Nobody seems to get what they expect: from Peter to Pilate, from Caiaphas to Mary Magdalene. If we don't get how surprising it all is, we've begun to lose our grip on the story, probably out of over-familiarity with at least some of its elements.

**So, at heart, you're trying to give us a sense of what it might truly have been like to be there.**

That's it. Firstly, I gathered together everything that seemed clear about the events. And that included things that might not be immediately obvious. For example, we know that John Mark's father has passed away because Luke refers to where he lives as Mary's house in Acts 12. Given that knowledge, I think it's fair to draw a picture of him as I have done here.

When so many centuries have passed by, it's easy to feel a sense of distance and to treat the story simply as a place to find lessons about faith and life. But these events took place. People's lives played out with all their hopes and doubts, their faith and fears. I wanted to give people today a chance to sense what it could have been like if only we had been able to be there.

# Study questions for groups

## Session 1: Looking over the edge

Palm Sunday can be viewed in several ways as Thomas observes at the start of this book. As a disciple, he's best known for his doubt which is a bit harsh on him. When Thomas says that he will not believe the resurrection without evidence, he is making a fair point. So it might be sensible to see him as one of the hard-headed realists among the followers.

Read Mark 11:1–11.

Then take a look at how Thomas is imagined seeing the events of Palm Sunday on pp. 17–21.

Talk about it using the following questions/prompts as required.

1 When an event is going well, are you an optimist enjoying it or a pessimist wondering what might go wrong? Are both sorts of personalities needed?

2 Are the events of Palm Sunday good news or bad news?

3 The details about the Palm Sunday entry into Jerusalem seem to have been a tightly guarded secret, probably not fully known even to all of the close disciples. Do you like to be thoroughly in charge of what's going on or are you happy to just get on with a small part? Can the desire to know and understand everything be a weakness? Or is it a strength?

4  As the day unfolds, the situation seems to be running out of control. When Jesus replies to the Pharisees' request to calm things down, he answers, 'If you silence the people, the very stones will cry out.' Are the authorities right to see Jesus as a threat?

5  Do you learn anything particular about Jesus from the Palm Sunday story? If this was all you'd seen and heard about him, how would you describe him?

6  Put yourself in Jesus' position. How do you think this day felt like for him?

## Session 2: Hitting hard

The gospel of Matthew is the most Jewish of the gospels but Matthew himself lived for a good while hated by his own people. That was because he collected taxation for the Romans who occupied their land. If any disciple might be expected to understand the tensions of life in Jerusalem, it was surely him.

Read Mark 12:38–43.

Then read pp. 60–62 of the book which imagines Matthew's reactions to what happens on the Wednesday before Passover.

You might also want to have a Bible open at Matthew 23 to refer to, if needed.

Talk about what happens using the following questions/prompts as required.

1  The first criticism of the authorities here is that they create heavier burdens for people to carry than they need to. When have you seen that happen? Do we ever make life more difficult for others?

2  Another criticism is of leaders who love being the centre of attention. What is wrong in that behaviour? Is it always wrong to enjoy the spotlight?

3  Jesus calls on those listening to be servants. Can you think of at least three good things about being a servant to others? More if you can!

4  Both Jesus and Paul speak out against making rules too detailed. Is that true of government? What about us? Can we do anything about it?

5  When Jesus calls some leaders 'whitewashed tombs', he's pointing out the difference between looking good and being good. But doesn't everyone hide behind their image a bit? Can we change that in our lives?

6  After teaching, Jesus sits down and watches for a while. That's when he notices the widow making her gift. How do we manage to balance doing things and learning through simply watching?

# Session 3: Near the fire

Peter's denial of Jesus is recorded in all four gospels.

Read John 18:15–17; 25–27 and Mark 14:66–72 to get a picture of it. The other disciple mentioned is generally accepted to be John.

Take a look now at the story as imagined on pp. 99–103.

Talk about it using the following questions/prompts as required.

1 When the disciples ran away from Gethsemane, it's easy to assume they scattered in panic. Instead, it seems that two followed the arrest party back to Jerusalem while the others continued to Bethany. In short, they sorted things out even in the heat of a crisis. Could you have been that brave and organised? What can we learn for our own lives together from this?

2 John gains entry into the courtyard because he is known to the servants and he gets Peter in as well. How difficult is it for us when we have to take a secondary role or depend on connections with someone better known? Do we react badly or well? How can we improve?

3 John is with people he knows while Peter is the outsider in the courtyard. How do you cope when with people you don't know? What do you do?

4 You could argue that Peter has no reason to panic. The servant girl clearly knows that John is a Jesus follower as she asks Peter if he's one too. Do we panic too easily? Do we get tempted to hide our faith? Why?

5   The problem with a lie is you get stuck with it and feel obliged to repeat it, as Peter does. In fact, his denial becomes more of a drama as it gets repeated. Do we ever over-dramatise when we find ourselves in a weak position? How do we get back from hiding the truth to telling it?

6   Peter surely feels at the end of this night that there is no way back, especially after seeing Jesus look at him (Luke 22:61). Do we find it difficult to believe forgiveness is possible for some people or even for some of the things we have done?

## Session 4: This time

What happened to bodies after a Roman crucifixion was often as grotesque as the execution itself. Without Joseph of Arimathea and Nicodemus, the Good Friday story would be even more hideous than it is.

Read Mark 15:42–47 and John 19:38–39.

Then look at what Joseph of Arimathea has to say as imagined on pp. 151–154.

Talk about it using the following questions/prompts as required.

1   The gospels report that Joseph was a good man who followed Jesus secretly because he was afraid. Why do you think he comes into the open?

2   When have you had to change your mind about something? Was it easy?

3   Joseph takes on a hard job. Talk about jobs you didn't want to do but had to. How did it feel?

4   In the retelling Joseph says, 'There comes a moment when you can't keep quiet anymore.' When should we speak up and when should we stay silent?

5   Joseph gives his tomb to Jesus. Share your thoughts and feelings about something that was intended for you and you gave away.

6   This is a story of someone who waited until it seemed to be too late. What things should you have done earlier?

7   Think of five words to describe how Joseph might have felt through the day?

## Session 5: The young man

The women that Mary Magdalene leaves behind at the tomb when she runs to fetch Peter and John include at least one surprising follower. Joanna is the wife of Chuza who is in charge of King Herod's household. Luke tells us that Jesus had healed her and she was one of the team that provided support to him.

Read Luke 24:2–7 and Mark 16:8.

Then take a look at the story on pp. 171–173.

Talk about it using the following questions/prompts as required.

1 The women at the tomb are described by the gospel writers as 'bewildered, trembling, afraid yet filled with joy'. That's quite a mix! To understand better what they were going through, share some moments of your own when your life was filled with conflicting emotions.

2 This part of the Easter story starts with the women being afraid and, in spite of the joy they feel, it ends with fear reasserting itself. How do we cope with fear? Why does it take over so easily sometimes?

3 In Matthew's account, the messenger from God tells them not to be afraid; then he adds 'take a look'. The problem seems to be that seeing isn't quite the same as believing. Why does that happen? Does it happen to us?

4 One of the things that is often missed about this incident is how gently the message is given. It starts with reassurance and is designed to encourage belief. Do we think enough about our tone of voice, how we say things and whether what we say will encourage a good response? How can we improve?

5 It's clear from Mark's gospel that the women don't go directly to the disciples with their message. Did they do a good thing in taking a pause? What do you think most worried them about sharing their message?

6 Talk about a time when you were scared to share a message you had. What happened? What did you learn?

## Session 6: His voice

The meeting between Jesus and Mary Magdalene outside the tomb is one of the best-known parts of the Bible. Mary was a leader among the team who supported Jesus. Her nickname literally means Tower, and as the Galilean town of Magdala does not appear to have existed in the time of Jesus, it's most likely that her nickname is a reference to her height. Luke tells us (8:1–3) that she had her demons but that Jesus drove them out. It's small wonder then that she cared so much for him.

Read John 20:11–17.

Then look at the scene through Mary's eyes on pp. 185–187.

Talk about the situation using the following questions/ prompts as required

1   It feels as if Mary stays in the garden to be alone in her grief and to cry freely. When have you needed space like that? And when have you sought out the company of others in the dark times?

2   Are there ways in which we help or hinder those experiencing sorrow?

3   We see what we want to see some days. It's no surprise that Mary thought she was speaking to the gardener. Think about a time when you totally misread a situation. What did you learn from it?

4 One word changes everything – 'Mary' – when someone who loves you calls, it makes all the difference in the world. Talk about times when someone called and you responded.

5 People rarely consider how brave it was of Mary to clasp hold of someone she must surely have doubted was there at all. What would you have done?

6 Jesus tells Mary she cannot 'hold on' to him (NIV, NRSV, GNB) or 'cling to him' (ESV, MSG). Sometimes the greatest challenge is letting go and moving on to the next challenge. Mary does it. Do we?

# Book group questions

1   What one thing struck you most when you read *Easter Inside Out*?

2   The balance of power in this story is complicated and unpredictable. Caiaphas famously declares, 'It is better for one man to die for the people than for a whole nation to be destroyed.' What did you feel you learnt about politics and power from this book? Why do we sometimes justify behaviour that perhaps we shouldn't?

3   Much of the story takes place in Jerusalem. Bartimaeus, who is new to the city, says it 'felt like a tight-packed, tough, unremitting place'. How would you describe it?

4   An early draft of this book was called *Dead Men Don't Eat Fish*. That was because it takes the sight of the risen Jesus eating food in the room in front of the disciples to finally convince them. But could it be a good thing to be sceptical? Is that what makes faith strong in the long run?

5   Who do you think you are most like in the Easter story and why?

6   If you were making a film of *Easter Inside Out*, which three scenes would you most enjoy bringing to the screen?

7   Who would you recommend this book to and why?

# 'Yet to Go'

*This isn't how it finishes;*
*This isn't where we end.*
*Short or long, there's paths to take*
*And words to say and injuries to mend.*

*It looked so dark for Mary*
*As she wept beside the tomb:*
*If only she could turn back time*
*To when hope filled each room.*

*She hears his voice, isn't sure.*
*If she blinks, will he be gone?*
*That's why Mary reached out*
*And desperately held on.*

*But morning in that garden*
*Could never be the end;*
*A story to be shared*
*Needs families and friends.*

*Our shoes should be love walking,*
*Our voice a healing sound,*
*Till we're in the arms of angels,*
*Our feet on holy ground.*

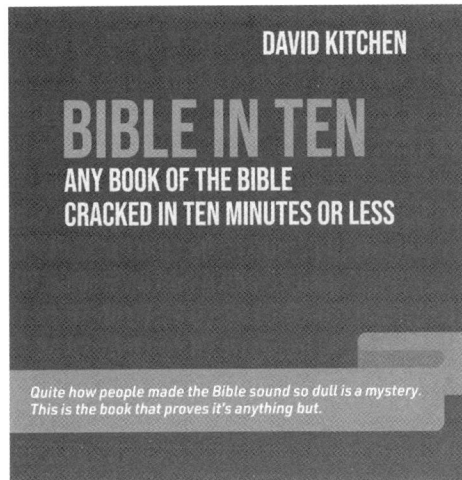

**DAVID KITCHEN**

# BIBLE IN TEN

## ANY BOOK OF THE BIBLE
## CRACKED IN TEN MINUTES OR LESS

*Quite how people made the Bible sound so dull is a mystery.
This is the book that proves it's anything but.*

*Bible in Ten* is for everyone who wants to be connected with all that is unexpected, beautiful and astonishing in the Bible. It tells the stories of success and failure, suffering and hope, home and exile, and a love that is stronger than death. Here are 67 short, sharp snapshots covering every corner of a book that people sometimes don't know quite as well as they think they do. It's a way into a volume that is often on the shelves but far less frequently taken off them. The Bible is packed with advice, stories and promises that cry out to be heard. This book gives people a real chance to take the words off the page and into their own world.

**Bible in Ten**
*Any book of the Bible cracked in ten minutes or less*
David Kitchen
978 1 80039 151 2        £12.99

**brfonline.org.uk**

# BRF Ministries

*Inspiring people of all ages to grow in Christian faith*

BRF Ministries is the home of Anna Chaplaincy, Living Faith, Messy Church and Parenting for Faith

As a charity, our work would not be possible without fundraising and gifts in wills. To find out more and to donate, visit brf.org.uk/give or call +44 (0)1235 462305

Registered with
FUNDRAISING
**REGULATOR**